They Thought
for
Themselves

They Thought for Themselves

TEN AMAZING JEWS

SID ROTH

Previous ISBN 0-910267-02-2
Previously copyrighted © 1996 by Sid Roth; Reprinted 1999, 2002, 2005.

Paperback:

ISBN 10: 0-7684-2842-4
ISBN 13: 978-0-7684-2842-1

Hardcover:

ISBN 10: 0-7684-3135-2
ISBN 13: 978-0-7684-3135-3

For Worldwide Distribution, Printed in the U.S.A.

48 49 50 51 52 53 / 22 21 20

Dedication

To Joy

Contents

Introduction. 9

Chapter 1 By David Yaniv. 11
           Paralyzed... "Learn to Live With It!". 13

Chapter 2 By Jonathan Bernis. 31
           No Place for a Good Jewish Boy. 33

Chapter 3 By Rose Price. 55
           The Survivor. 57

Chapter 4 By Alyosha Ryabinov. 75
           A New Song. 77

Chapter 5 By Sharon R. Allen. 89
           Yiddishkeit. 91

Chapter 6 By Sid Roth. 113
           There Must Be Something More!. 115

Chapter 7 By Michael L. Brown, Ph.D.. 137
           Tradition or Truth? What I Learned
           About Rabbinic Judaism. 139

Chapter 8 By Randy and Tricia Horne. 165
           It Was Not for Me. 167

Chapter 9 By Batya Segal. 177
           Bat Shalom: Daughter of Zion. 179

Chapter 10 By Manny and Sandra Sheskin Brotman. 203
           The Amazing Jewish Book and the
           God-Shaped Hole in My Soul. 205

Introduction

My father was born in Poland into a traditional Jewish family. My mother's family, while also very Jewish, was much more Americanized. Dad won out in our religious education. I attended a traditional synagogue and was trained for bar mitzvah.

Even as a child, I saw the hypocrisy in our religious observance. For instance, on major holidays, we parked several blocks away from the shul because we didn't want the rabbi to know we drove on the Shabbat. And we had to get there early or the other members would take all the best parking spaces.

The long services in Hebrew, a language I didn't understand, added to my boredom and resentment. Why did we go to synagogue? Why all the ritual? Why was God not speaking to us today? Was the Bible from God? These are just a few of the questions that plagued me.

❖ 9 ❖

I was proud of being a Jew, but the religious side turned me off. It just wasn't relevant.

For almost 30 years, God was irrelevant to me—until I thought for myself.

This book is the result of a dream I had in which I was instructed to find and interview Jewish people who broke through the mold of their previous experiences to achieve their destiny. Everyone has a special destiny, but few reach it.

The people in this book come from widely divergent backgrounds including a holocaust survivor, a concert pianist, a media executive, and a Ph.D. They range in upbringing from atheistic to Orthodox.

What is the common denominator among those in this unusual group?

They all thought for themselves…and dared to confront the forbidden.

If you have ever thought that there must be something more to life, you were right!

CHAPTER 1
BY DAVID YANIV

CHAPTER 1

Paralyzed... "Learn to Live With It!"

I was born in Tel Aviv in 1936 to parents who immigrated from Germany. My parents kept up tradition, celebrating Yom Kippur, Rosh Hashanah, and other holidays, but they were never really religious. After the Second World War, when my father found out that two of his sisters and one brother and their families had been killed in Nazi Germany, he took every Bible and everything in our home that was even remotely religious and threw it out. "Where was God?" he would ask. "How could God allow such a thing to happen?" From then on, I was raised in an atheistic home. My father even resisted my having a bar mitzvah. Although he finally allowed it, he refused to set foot in the synagogue.

> **"How could god allow
> such a thing to happen?"**

In 1960 I married a South African girl named Sheila, whom I met when she and her mother came to Israel as tourists. At the time, I was a guide and a bus driver. Her mother, who took two tours with me, one day said, "My baby is waiting for me in Haifa. I want you to meet her." I thought it was funny that this elderly woman would have a baby. But when I reached Haifa and saw her "baby," I realized she was a matchmaker. Sheila and I went to South Africa on our honeymoon to visit her family—and stayed twelve and one-half years.

I'm a refrigeration and air-conditioning engineer by trade. I did quite well in business in South Africa for a time. Then I undertook a project to air condition a large building. The quantity surveyor I hired to estimate the cost of the job made a mistake, and I lost all my money.

My lawyer told me it was useless to sue the surveyor because he wasn't insured. And even though I was bankrupt, I had to finish the job because I had signed a contract.

The Mistake Paralyzed Me for Life

Afterward, I decided to return to Israel. Moving back was very difficult for my wife, but she realized it was best for us and our two sons, who were 11 and 8 years old. At the time, I spoke Hebrew, but my family did not. We decided to live on a *moshav*, which is an agricultural commune similar to a *kibbutz*.

I thought we would stay there for a short time to allow my family to learn Hebrew, and then I would find work in my trade. But when the time came, and I said, "All right, let's move to the big town," they didn't want to go. They had come to love life on the moshav. Even if they had agreed, however, it would have been difficult to leave. You can't build up any savings there because you only receive a small monthly allowance to buy food and supplies. But if we stayed at the moshav, we were set for life.

The first year on the moshav we had to work in different jobs to allow everyone to get to know us and for us to get to know them. Toward the end of that year I was assigned to milk the cows. I enjoyed it because it was something new and because I knew it was just a temporary assignment.

> **The first year on the moshav
> we had to work in different jobs
> to allow everyone to get to know
> us and for us to get to know them.**

One day in the cow shed I slipped on a wet spot on the floor and fell flat on my back. My back was in so much pain I went to the hospital to have it checked. The hospital technicians didn't find anything serious on the x-rays. They said, "You just got a good knock there. Go home, rest, take some painkillers, and it will be all right within two weeks."

Instead of getting better, the pain got worse. The second time I went to the hospital, they x-rayed me again, and again sent me home saying there was nothing wrong. I rested for another two weeks, and by that time the pain was excruciating. I had never experienced such pain. The painkillers helped initially, but after a while they lost their effect. I kept increasing the dosage until I was taking 50 pills a day for three years.

I reached a point where every morning when I got out of bed my feet would go numb. I knew something was seriously wrong, but I also knew I couldn't go back to that same hospital again.

Because of the bureaucracy in Israel it took some connections to be allowed to go to another hospital, but through friends who knew somebody who knew somebody, it was arranged for me to visit another hospital in Tel Aviv. The doctors there did a special x-ray called a myelogram.

After the x-ray, the head of the neurosurgical department himself came to me and said, "You've got two slipped discs, one of which is completely compressed and the other one is missing a piece." He was amazed I had waited so long to get help.

When I asked for his prognosis, he replied, "Well, we'll have to operate."

"What does that entail?" I asked, cautiously.

"Oh, it's nothing," he said. "Ten days and you're back home as good as new."

That sounded wonderful to me, so I said, "Let's do it."

When I woke up from the anesthetic in the evening after the operation, I had no feeling from my waist down, so I called for a doctor. The doctor on the evening shift said, "I can't tell you anything. You will have to wait until the morning when all the surgeons come in for the day shift."

> **When I woke up from the anesthetic in the evening after the operation, I had no feeling from my waist down.**

The next morning the doctor who had operated came to me and said, "David, I'm terribly sorry. I've got some bad news for you."

Bracing myself, I asked, "What do you mean you've got bad news for me?"

He said, "I made a mistake, and you will be paralyzed for life."

Apparently, he had cut too deeply with his scalpel and severed the nerves that were essential for me to walk. I had no feeling in one leg and only partial feeling in the other.

At first I was in shock. Then I began to feel sorry for myself. I thought, *What am I going to do now? I had pain before, but at least I could walk. If I could only take time back now, I would rather live with the pain.* But I couldn't go back.

A Broken Man

The doctor's prognosis for the future was summed up in one cold sentence: "Learn to live with it." It was very difficult. I hated everybody. I blamed everybody. But worst of all, I absolutely hated myself. I could not accept what had happened.

From the hospital I was sent to a convalescent home called Beth-Levinshtein, which helps paralyzed people, mainly soldiers who get wounded in the war. They also take some private cases, such as mine. There I started to feel a little better about myself because everyone around me was either worse off than I was or in the same condition. The staff made iron calipers (braces) for me which were attached to special shoes. With the help of crutches and the calipers, I could make my way around without a wheelchair, although it was very difficult.

> **But worst of all, I absolutely hated myself. I could not accept what had happened.**

Three and one-half months later, I returned to the moshav to find my home rearranged. My friends had made a ramp so I could easily get into the house with my wheelchair. They installed handles in the bathroom and other places around the house where I would need them. I was very grateful.

But now that I was surrounded by healthy, active people, I began to realize how much of an invalid I was. I started feeling sorry for myself again, so much so that I needed psychiatric treatment. Never in a million years would I have ever thought I would need a psychiatrist. I had always been such a strong person. Suddenly, I was a broken man.

> **Suddenly, I was a broken man.**

Before long, the psychiatrist gave up on me because I wouldn't stop feeling sorry for myself. I was the most unhappy person imaginable. I couldn't forgive the doctor. I couldn't forgive anyone.

My condition was also very difficult for my wife, to the point that I was afraid she might leave me. She never did. In fact, she would try to reassure me, telling me not to worry, that she would stay with me through thick and thin. But the more she told me not to worry, the more I worried.

The moshav gave me an easy job in the office where my coworkers were especially kind. But the nicer they were, the worse I felt. I was sure they were giving me special treatment because of my disabilities.

In the midst of my pity parties, I still had hope that I would some day walk again. I read in the newspaper one day about a man who would put his hand on sick people, sending something that felt like an electric current through their bodies, and they would feel better. The moshav offered to pay my expenses, so I went to him. Nothing happened.

Then I heard about a guru. I went to him with the same result. I believed in each one I went to. When you're as desperate as I was, you try anything. The moshav even paid for transcendental meditation. Nothing worked.

Nothing happened.
Nothing worked.

After seven and one-half years of trying everything the world had to offer, I finally gave up. I finally accepted the expert advice of all the specialists, professors, and neuro-surgeons who told me: "Learn to live with it. You are going to remain paralyzed for the rest of your life. Don't even think of getting better." My wife had long since given up hope that my condition would ever improve. She would say, "What are you running after? Accept it. This is how you are going to remain. I've accepted it. Why can't you?"

And, at that point, I really did accept it. I still felt sorry for myself, but I accepted it. I realized that nobody could help me. I determined to go on and try to live as normal a life as I possibly could.

Why Don't You Pray With Me?

One day, I stayed home from work with the flu and was totally bored. At two o'clock that afternoon I decided to watch television. Since Israeli stations only broadcast in the evening, I started watching a program on Lebanese television called *The 700 Club*. I was intrigued by the name, thinking it was an entertainment program.

I soon realized that it was a Christian show. But there was nothing else to do, and I was curious, so I kept watching. Still, I felt like I was doing something wrong, so I locked the door. I didn't want my wife and my children to catch me watching Christian television.

The program held my interest because it featured stories about people who were healed from different sicknesses. The first time I watched, there was an interview with a woman who had been healed of cancer. She showed an x-ray of a tumor the size of an orange. Then she showed an x-ray of the same spot taken three days later. The tumor had disappeared.

I was sure it was phony. These people had to be paid actors. Some of the stories even made me laugh out loud at the absurdity of the claims. Yet, I found myself watching every day at two o'clock—behind locked doors.

After a month of this, I decided to tell my wife. I said, "Sheila, I've been watching this Christian program about people who get healed by believing in Jesus and by people praying for them."

I expected her to be annoyed with me. On the contrary, she said, "If it makes you feel better, keep watching." She even suggested I record it so we could watch it together in the evening.

During every program there was a time when co-host Ben Kinchlow would say, "Pray with me." Whenever it came to that part, I switched off the television. I didn't even want to hear people pray to Jesus. I felt it was wrong.

> **Whenever it came to that part, I switched off the television. I didn't even want to hear people pray to Jesus. I felt it was wrong.**

As I was watching alone one afternoon several months later, it seemed that Ben's finger stretched out from the television pointing straight at me. He said, "You! Why don't you pray with me?" I could have sworn he was talking directly to me. I got scared. The next thing I knew, I found myself praying the sinner's prayer with him. Here I was praying with him to this "Jesus," who to me had never been more than a dirty name. When that prayer was finished, I couldn't believe what I had done. I thought to myself, *What on earth do I do now?*

I immediately told Sheila. Again, she responded more positively than I expected. She said, "If it makes you feel good, you just carry on. But do me a favor. Don't tell anyone about it. Let it be between us for now."

I was sure that I was the only Jewish person in the whole world who had ever prayed that prayer. I thought, *The first thing I have to do is buy a full Bible.* So I went to Nazareth and bought a Bible. At the book store, I saw a map of the city on display, and, somehow, the name of a Baptist church caught my eye.

As I started reading my Bible, I soon discovered there was more to it than I had ever imagined. I found that the prophecies from the Old Testament are fulfilled in the New

Testament. And I started to wonder why Jewish people throughout the centuries had not believed in Jesus.

You Will Be Healed

The following Sunday, I went to the Baptist church at eight o'clock in the morning. I was too early—the doors were locked.

All around me I heard the bells of churches ringing, and here this church was locked! I was just about to leave when an Arab man walked up and introduced himself as the pastor. He first spoke to me in Arabic and then English, because he didn't speak Hebrew. When I told him my story, he was amazed. He said, "We've tried to get Jewish people to come to the Lord for years, and here you're walking in yourself. This is the first time since I've been a pastor that this has happened."

The pastor invited me to stay for the service. Being Jewish in an Arab congregation, I thought I would feel out of place, but I didn't. The love I experienced that day was the love of Jesus.

> **The love I experienced that day was the love of Jesus.**

At the end of the service there was an invitation to come forward to receive the Lord as personal savior. After I came forward, I found myself praying the same prayer I had been praying daily for four and one-half months in front of my television. But this time I did it in front of a whole congregation of witnesses.

This was almost too much for my wife. It was one thing to watch a Christian program or pray a prayer in private. It was quite another to make a public profession of faith in Jesus. She was incensed that I would do such a thing without first consulting her.

However, as the weeks went by and she saw that I was steadfast in my decision, she agreed to come with me to a meeting of Jewish believers. Soon afterward, she accepted Jesus too.

About five months after I became a believer in the Messiah, I was again watching *The 700 Club* when co-host Danuta Soderman had a word of knowledge. She said, "There is someone," she didn't specifically say where, "who has been paralyzed halfway down his body for years," and with me that was the case, seven and one-half years. She said, "He will feel a warm sensation running through his body, and he will be healed."

I said, "Oh, please, God, let it be me." I believed it was me, but nothing happened. Still I kept praying because I realized immediately if it wasn't for me, it must have been for someone else.

> **...all of a sudden a feeling like an electric current ran from my spine down to my tiptoes, and my feet started jumping 40 inches at a time.**

That same evening around ten o'clock I was lying in bed reading my Bible, when all of a sudden a feeling like an electric current ran from my spine down to my tiptoes, and my feet started jumping 40 inches at a time.

When people are paralyzed, they get unwanted reflex movements, and I thought that was what this was. Some of them were more severe than others, but I couldn't explain the electric shock. Finally, the movements stopped, and I went to sleep.

The next morning when I woke up, I started to assist my legs with my hands as I usually did in order to get them out of bed. As I touched my legs, all of a sudden I realized I had feeling in them! I thought, *Wait a minute. This is unusual!* I started to touch all the places where I had lost feeling years before. There was feeling in them!

I shouted, "Sheila, for God's sake, come here! I can feel!"

"Rubbish," she said. "Lie down." She took a needle and started pricking me. "Close your eyes. Where am I pricking you?" And she continued pricking me in different places on my legs. Each time she pricked my legs, I told her the correct spot. Now she began to share my excitement.

Immediately, I went to the dispensary on our moshav to see the doctor. I put the special shoes back on because I still didn't know exactly what had happened to me, and, after seven and one-half years of paralysis, my legs had no muscles in them. When our moshav doctor was shocked too, I realized a true miracle had occurred.

When our moshav doctor was shocked too, I realized a true miracle had occurred.

The moshav doctor sent me to a hospital for an electric test of my reflexes. I had had this test done many times before, and, of course, it was always negative. This time my reflexes responded to the test perfectly. The doctor who performed the test asked if I could return the following week.

A week later, I met with about 25 doctors, neurosurgeons, and neurologists from all over the country, including the neurosurgeon who had operated on me. They all examined me, but no one could give a logical explanation for what had happened. They said it was not possible. Some of them even thought I was lying by claiming that the older x-rays were mine. Even today, doctors who examine them cannot believe that I am walking.

At the end of the examination they said to me, "This is a medical miracle."

I said, "Listen. This is not a medical miracle. This is *Yeshua* (Jesus)."

Someone asked, "Yeshua who?" Yeshua is a very common name in Israel, so he thought perhaps Yeshua was my physiotherapist, or a friend.

> I said, "Listen. This is
> not a medical miracle.
> This is *Yeshua* (Jesus)."

"Yeshua the Messiah," I responded.

That was too much for these Jewish doctors. They did not want to hear another word about this "Jesus."

They refused to believe He could have had anything to do with my healing. We know from the Bible that even when people saw Jesus perform miracles right before their eyes, they didn't believe. Some even accused Him of being demon possessed.

The doctor said to take off the iron calipers, but to keep using the crutches because my legs were just skin and bones. And slowly, slowly, I took my first steps in seven and one-half years. I knelt down on knees that hadn't felt anything since the accident and thanked the Lord for the miracle He had done.

But He wasn't finished yet. The doctors had told me that the muscles in my legs were all dead and that they would never grow back. Over time, God recreated those muscles. Today, my feet are just as normal as anyone else's.

You Have to Leave

When the members of the moshav saw me walking, they didn't accept that this was the work of Yeshua any more than the doctors did. Instead, they chose to believe the doctors' conclusion that it was a "medical miracle."

It was not long before word had spread around the moshav that I was a believer in Yeshua. The leaders of the moshav called me into their office and said, "We're terribly sorry, but you have to leave. We do not accept Christians on the moshav." This moshav is associated with B'nai B'rith in New York, and they were worried they would lose their funding if they didn't expel me.

I said, "I call myself a 'Messianic Jew,' and I will not go quietly. There is a great big Christian world out there just waiting to hear my story."

Sensing that the publicity generated by expelling me might be worse than if they let me stay, they said I could remain—*if* I promised I would not evangelize on the moshav.

> I said, "I call myself a 'Messianic Jew,' and I will not go quietly. There is a great big Christian world out there just waiting to hear my story."

That arrangement worked fine until May 1988 when I participated in a major Messianic Jewish event in Jerusalem called "Shavuot '88"—at that time the largest gathering of Jewish believers in Israel in almost two thousand years. It seemed that every Hebrew-speaking newspaper in Jerusalem covered the miracle of my healing.

When I came home from the meetings, the moshav leaders said, "That's it. You promised us you would not evangelize. Now your picture is splashed all over the newspapers. B'nai B'rith is going to stop the money flowing to us. You have to leave."

They voted us out at a general meeting and gave us ten days in which to leave. Nobody from the moshav, where we had lived for 16 years, even came to help us pack our belongings.

If God had not made a way, we would have been out in the street and penniless. But we serve a living God! At the gathering somebody had handed me an envelope. As I ripped it open, I couldn't believe my eyes! It contained a scholarship and airline tickets to attend Bible school in Dallas, Texas.

My wife and I graduated in May 1989 and followed the Lord's leading to Seattle, where we live today. I have been healed for well over a decade, and my faith grows deeper every day. Soon we will return to Israel and proclaim the good news about the true Messiah who saves and heals!

Commentary by Sid Roth

I read in the Torah that God heals people. But in 30 years of going to a traditional synagogue I never saw anyone get healed. On television I saw "faith healers" and thought they were all counterfeit. But you can't have a good counterfeit unless there is the real thing. The Talmud, as well as the New

Testament, records healings that occurred when Jewish believers in Jesus prayed to God. The Talmud also warns traditional Jews not to let Messianic Jews (Jewish believers in Jesus) pray for them (Tosefta Chullin, Chapter 2:22-23). This is a backhanded compliment! These rabbis recognized that the Jewish followers of Jesus had power to heal in His Name. And once you experience healing in His Name, you might believe in Him. Isaiah 53:4-5 tells us the Messiah would bear away all our diseases.

But only our diseases did He bear Himself, and our pains carried: while we indeed esteemed Him stricken, smitten of God, and afflicted. Yet He was wounded for our transgressions, He was bruised for our iniquities: the chastisement for our peace was upon Him; and through His bruises was healing granted to us.

The early Messianic Jews, even brand-new believers, experienced miracles of healing in His Name. And since He doesn't change, I too have seen many Jewish people healed in Jesus' Name. My own mother, before becoming a Messianic Jew, was healed in His Name.

CHAPTER 2
BY JONATHAN BERNIS

CHAPTER 2

No Place for a Good Jewish Boy

I was raised in a traditional Jewish home. I refer to myself as a former "holiday Jew." We went to synagogue on the high holidays and had family gatherings on the important holidays like Passover, Rosh Hashanah, and Yom Kippur, the Day of Atonement.

I was forced against my will to go to both Hebrew school and religious school. So while my friends were out playing on Tuesdays and Thursdays after school, I was studying Hebrew in the synagogue to prepare for the most important experience a Jewish young man can go through—the Bar Mitzvah, becoming a son of the commandment. And so at age 13, I was Bar Mitzvah and entered into adulthood. At that time my parents felt they had fulfilled their responsibility, and they gave me the choice whether to continue on with synagogue life or not. I had had enough of Hebrew school and religious school, and so I departed from the synagogue except for the high holidays.

> **I remember asking some of my teachers, "We're the chosen people, but what are we chosen for?"**

As I reflect back on the things that I learned growing up, I had quite a rich heritage. I learned all about the patriarchs of our faith, Abraham, Isaac and Jacob, and I learned about the calling of the Jewish people. I was taught that we were chosen people and that we had a special relationship with God. But I never really quite understood. I remember asking some of my teachers, "We're the chosen people, but what are we chosen for?" One teacher responded that we were chosen to be persecuted. That wasn't something I was too excited about.

I remember being taught about Moses and how he had this divine encounter with the burning bush and how he led the children of Israel out of Egypt. I learned that the Passover, the Exodus out of Egypt, is probably the watershed event in Jewish history. It is the most important holiday that we celebrate. And I fondly remember sitting together as a family and reciting the story of the Passover Exodus. I heard all about the God of Israel. But one thing that I didn't learn was how to have a relationship with God. I remember asking what God was like, and none of my teachers could give me an answer.

At that time I had a great fear of dying. I went to my rabbi and asked, "Rabbi, what happens after you die?" He gave me a long answer about this man climbing a mountain and not being able to see the other side. When he finally reaches the top, then he can see the other side. He said that God is already at the top of the mountain looking over the other side. I left the rabbi's office amazed at his wisdom, but having no idea what he meant. I was more confused than before. Years later, as I thought about that encounter I realized the rabbi had no idea how to answer my question. He was just too proud to admit it.

From the time I was a little boy I learned a prayer called the *Shema*, which is found in Deuteronomy 6:4, "*Shema Israel Adonai Elohenu Adonai echad, Hear O Israel, the Lord our God, the Lord is one.*" I was taught that we Jews were responsible for bringing the revelation of the one true God to the world and that this was something of which we could be proud. We believed in the God of Abraham, Isaac, and Jacob, the God of Israel. From the time I was knee high, I learned to recite that prayer, the central confession of Judaism.

> **I heard all about the God of Israel. But one thing that I didn't learn was how to have a relationship with God.**

In spite of all this, I learned more about what Jews *did not* believe than what Jews *did* believe. I learned that Jews do *not* believe in Jesus. That was made very, very clear to me. I was taught that the Christians were responsible for the holocaust, for the Crusades, for the pogroms, for all the terrible persecutions of Jewish people. My understanding was that anyone who wasn't Jewish was a Christian. A Gentile, a Christian, it made no difference to me. They were non-Jews.

> **I learned more about what Jews *did not* believe than what Jews *did* believe. I learned that Jews do *not* believe in Jesus.**

I grew up with what I refer to as an "us versus them" mentality. As Jews we had the God of Abraham, Isaac, and Jacob. On the other side was Christianity. There was the religious institution of Judaism and the religious institution of Christianity. Christians had three gods. Their central deity, as I understood it, was Jesus Christ, son of Mr. and Mrs. Christ. I thought that Jesus was His first name and Christ was His last name. That was all confusing to me.

I remember visiting a Catholic church with a friend as a young teenager. The priest was standing in the pulpit with all these goblets and smoke rising around him. And there was a statue of Jesus Christ and a couple of other gods. It didn't make much sense to this good Jewish boy.

I understood that as Jews we had the synagogue and the temple, and on the Christian side they had the cathedral, the church, and the monastery. We had the Star of David on our flag, the religious symbol of our people. The

Christians had their own symbol called the cross. There was no relationship between the two whatsoever. I was taught that we had our book called the Torah, the five books of Moses and the writings of the Jewish prophets, a book that Christians call the Old Testament. And they had another book called the New Testament. This was the book of the Christians.

In my view, the two religions had nothing in common except for one thing—Christians embraced our book. I was pretty happy about that. I didn't believe in the Christian Bible, but Christians believed in the Jewish Scriptures.

I was brought up believing in the Jewish holidays. We had Rosh Hashanah, the Jewish New Year, Yom Kippur, the Day of Atonement, Passover, Hanukkah, and all the other Jewish holidays. The Christians had Christmas, Lent, and Easter.

We had matzo, gefilte fish, and kreplach. They had Easter eggs, chocolate bunnies, and Christmas trees. We had our menorah that we lit on Hanukkah. They had the little baby in the manger. On the one hand I saw this picture of the Christian God hanging on the cross eternally. Then during Christmas He was transformed into this eternal infant. It was very confusing.

> **In my view, the two religions had nothing in common except for one thing— Christians embraced our book.**

We had our rabbis and Christians had their priests, pastors, and monks. We had our religion, they had theirs, and there was a gulf and a wall between the two. The idea was very clearly expressed in all the teaching that I received that Jews are not to believe in Jesus. Judaism and Christianity were two distinct religions with nothing in common. Never the two shall meet. That is the mentality of most Jewish people, and that's what I was raised to understand and believe.

I Knew Christians Were "Dangerous" People

In high school, my preconceived notions about Christians and Christianity were seriously challenged. The assistant coach of our wrestling team was different from anyone I had ever met. Besides being an all-American wrestler, he was part of a group called Athletes in Action and the leader of a high school outreach called Young Life.

> **I was convinced that all born-again Christians were hypocrites. I knew they were "dangerous" people who we were supposed to avoid.**

This man was always smiling. I could not figure out why. No matter what people said to him or what comments they made about him, he was always smiling. Word quickly circulated around the high school, "Stay away from this guy; he's one of those born-again Christians."

By this time I was convinced that all born-again Christians were hypocrites. I knew they were "dangerous" people who we were supposed to avoid. But there were some things about this man that I could not figure out. First of all I couldn't deny that he was probably the nicest person that I'd ever met. I couldn't deny that he had great joy, something that I didn't have. I was happy some days; other days I was miserable. He was always happy. But what impressed me the most about him was that he had a sense of purpose, a sense of destiny. He knew where he had come from and where he was going. He knew that God had put him on this earth for a purpose. He didn't have any fear of death. I was impressed by that. That drew me.

This coach started to share the Gospel with me and invited me to some of his Young Life meetings. I figured, *Why not? There are some beautiful girls who attend, and it looks like the thing to do.* A short time later he invited me to one of the Young Life camps down in Florida. I went for one reason and one reason only—he offered it to me free of charge. I thought, *I can go to Disney World and hang out on the beaches for free. Such a deal!*

So I went down to this camp and everything was going great. I was having a wonderful time—until I found out that part of the deal was I had to listen to the guest speaker every night. One speaker began to share about Jesus Christ, the God of the Christians. And for the first day, I was squirming in my seat and very uncomfortable. But as time went on, I was really drawn in by the things he had to say.

I marveled at the stories of this man Jesus who could walk on the water, heal the sick, raise the dead, and supernaturally provide food for a multitude. I thought, *This is really interesting*. And I noticed that there was something different about these messages than anything I had experienced growing up in the synagogue. The teaching in the synagogue seemed to go into my head, as head knowledge, but as this man spoke it was like something was happening in my heart. There was a churning and a drawing from my heart.

I was amazed at what was happening. I didn't know what to make of it. Later, I attended another Young Life camp. Again I felt a drawing. The speaker challenged those who hadn't made a decision to embrace Jesus to ask God to reveal Himself to them. He directed us to find a place of solitude where we could pray.

I noticed that there was something different about these messages than anything I had experienced growing up in the synagogue. The teaching in the synagogue seemed to go into my head, as head knowledge, but as this man spoke it was like something was happening in my heart. There was a churning and a drawing from my heart.

That was a real dilemma for me. I had never prayed before outside of using the prayer book. I knew how to read Hebrew and how to recite the prayers in the prayer books, but I had no idea how to spontaneously pray to God from my heart.

So I sat by a stream looking up at a beautiful clear sky with thousands of stars, not knowing how to pray to God. I said something like, "God, I believe You're real, and I've never spoken to You before, but I'm talking to You now. I really want to know You. If this Jesus is who they say He is, please show me. I really want to know. Amen." I returned to the meeting and watched as a number of my friends made a profession of faith in Jesus. And I saw their lives change before me. But there was a problem. Something in me said, *This is true, but I'm Jewish and Jews do not believe in Jesus.*

Eventually, I lost contact with my coach and lost interest in Jesus.

A Change in Plans

After I finished high school, I had one goal—to be a rich and successful businessman. I wanted to earn a million dollars before I was 30, to make my mark on the world as a worldwide industrialist, and retire early with multi-millions of dollars. So off I went to the University of Buffalo to earn a degree in business and start making as much money as possible as quickly as possible. God, however, had other ideas.

It was at college that I began experimenting with drugs, eastern meditation, and the occult. "Mind-expanding" drugs and the supernatural realm became a major pursuit around my business studies and occupied much of my free time. All of this radically changed with an encounter with a young woman I knew who was almost destroyed by drugs.

She quit going to class. She stopped caring about her appearance. Every time I saw her, she looked worse than before—her eyes bloodshot, her hands shaky, and her hair unkempt. There was nothing I, or anyone else, could do to bring her back from the brink of ruin and death. My relationship with her grew more distant because I couldn't watch her continue to destroy herself. Eventually, I lost contact with her.

You can imagine how shocked I was when I ran into her off campus one day and she looked completely well and healthy. Light sparkled in her eyes. When she saw me, the happy grin on her face got even bigger. Everything about her was different.

"I Have Been Born Again!"

Before I could think better of it, I blurted out, "What in the world happened to you?" I realize now how rude that sounds, but I really could not help myself. It was as though she had come back from the walking dead.

"I've been born again!" she said.

"You've been what?" I asked.

"Born again," she laughed. "I've made Jesus Christ the Lord of my life."

I could not deny the evidence standing right in front of me, but I did not want to accept what she was telling me. I thought, *If it worked for you, fine, but I have other plans for my life.*

She could tell from the puzzled look on my face that I wasn't making the connection, so she proceeded to tell me, with great enthusiasm, that she had turned to Jesus, and that He had set her free from her addiction. The desire had just gone away. One instant, she was a hopeless addict. The next, the craving had vanished.

I could not deny the evidence standing right in front of me, but I did not want to accept what she was telling me. I thought, *If it worked for you, fine, but I have other plans for my life.* I just wanted to get away from her, and that took at least ten minutes.

Even then, I couldn't really get away. For the next few weeks she called me every day, asking questions like, "Do you know *why* you're here on earth?" and "*Where* would you go if you died right now?"

At first, I politely tried to brush her off, but I was beginning to sense a certain pressure. Her questions haunted me. Why *was* I here? Where *would* I go if I died? Her words had impact because there was no denying that something amazing and real had happened to her. She was not the same person I had known before.

❖ 43 ❖

No Place for a Good Jewish Boy

After numerous invitations, I finally agreed to go with her to a home Bible study group that she belonged to. From the moment I walked into the room, I wanted to turn around and run. Clearly, this was no place for a good Jewish boy to be—especially one who was still using drugs. But I couldn't leave. At this time, my only mode of transportation was a Suzuki 750 motorcycle. It was a terrible, stormy night, complete with pouring and blowing rain. By the time I arrived at the Bible study, I was soaked to the skin.

The wife of the leader who was hosting the Bible study gave me some clothes to change into while my clothes tumbled around in her clothes dryer throughout the evening. I couldn't leave without my clothes!

> **I knew I was a sinner, since I was dealing and using drugs, but it was the first time in my life that I was aware of my physical separation from God.**

The study session seemed to go on for hours, although it was probably only around 90 minutes or so. I was miserable. I felt totally and completely out of place and was positive that everyone there was fully aware of my extreme discomfort. I'm sure you know how this feels—it is not a great feeling.

In addition to that, the leader approached me at the conclusion of the Bible study, and in a decidedly German accent, invited me to join him in the living room for a few minutes. You can imagine my horror from the moment I heard his very clear German accent addressing only me. After all, I had been brought up believing that the world was divided into two groups: Jews and Gentiles—and that Gentiles didn't like us very much—especially German Gentiles, based on the facts of the holocaust. I had a sub-conscious fear of all Germans, and I felt as though I was standing in the fiery furnace of that fear.

Nevertheless, I followed him to the living room and sat down on the couch where we were joined by an older gen-tleman. He placed a Bible on my lap and began to lead me through the Scriptures to Romans 3:23, "*For all have sinned and fall short of the glory of God.*" *Interesting.* I knew I was a sin-ner, since I was dealing and using drugs, but it was the first time in my life that I was aware of my physical separation from God. Then he took me over to Romans 6:23, which said, "*For the wages of sin is death, but the gift of God is eternal life in Christ Jesus our Lord.*"

At that moment, I had what can only be described as a supernatural experience. Although I did not have a vision or hear a heavenly voice, I do not know what else to call it. The room became abnormally bright and warm. I began to sweat profusely, and I can honestly say that I felt as though the couch I had been sitting on had arms that reached out and grabbed me—holding me in place.

I had begun to deal with a sense of my own separation from a God who *loved* me, Jonathan Bernis, 20-year-old col-lege student! It was that plain and simple! At the same time,

I struggled with an innate understanding that this direction meant abandoning my own goals and ambitions. Looking back at this event of more than 30 years ago, I am convinced that the presence of God came into the room that evening and apprehended me. God had a plan for my life that was different from my own, and He meant to make sure I would lay aside my plans and follow Him.

> **I am convinced that the presence of God came into the room that evening and apprehended me. God had a plan for my life that was different from my own, and He meant to make sure I would lay aside my plans and follow Him.**

I felt the weight of my sin. And then I was asked to pray a simple prayer repenting of my sin and inviting Jesus into my heart. By this time, I was so uncomfortable and there was such a battle going on inside of me, I would have prayed anything just to get out of that house. It wasn't very eloquent, but it was a sincere prayer of repentance.

As soon as I prayed that prayer, the lights and the temperature in the room returned to normal, the battle was finished and the couch released me. Then the teacher's wife brought in my folded, dry clothes and I was free to go. It was a very strange experience.

What Were the Jewish Heroes Doing in the Christian Bible?

Over the next few days, I developed a tremendous hunger for the Bible, but I did not have a Bible and did not know where to get one! I wanted to read the New Testament in particular, but where does a good Jewish boy go to shop for a New Testament? I could not go to my friends—they were all drug users. I could not go to the rabbi—he surely did not have one. I had no idea the Bible was the bestselling book of all time, and I could have bought one at any grocery store or pharmacy!

Finally I remembered that my high school wrestling coach had given me a Bible and said I would need it some day. I had thrown it into a box in my closet at home and forgotten about it.

Was there a parallel universe? Were there two Abrahams—a Christian Abraham and a Jewish Abraham, the father of all Jewish people? Was there a Christian David and a Jewish David? What about the other Jewish heroes? Was there a Jewish Isaac and a Christian parallel? Had they converted to Christianity and no one had ever told me?

I jumped on my motorcycle, drove over sixty miles to my parents' house, ran up to my room, and dug through the box in the closet until I found the Bible. I ran back out of the house without ever saying "hello" or "goodbye," and drove back to my dorm room, where I devoured the Scriptures. I couldn't get enough.

> **His name wasn't even Jesus, it was Yeshua. In Matthew it says His name would be called Yeshua, which means the "salvation of God" or "God saves," because He will save His people from their sins.**

I do not know what I expected to find in the New Testament. I had always thought of it as the Christians' book, and I didn't think there would be any connection at all to what I had learned at synagogue as a child.

You can imagine my shock when I dove into the book of Matthew and immediately found references to Abraham, Moses, David, and the other Jewish heroes I had learned about as a child. I couldn't understand, though, what these great figures of Judaism were doing in the Christian Bible. *Was there a parallel universe? Were there two Abrahams—a Christian Abraham and a Jewish Abraham, the father of all Jewish people? Was there a Christian David and a Jewish David? What about the other Jewish heroes? Was there a Jewish Isaac and a Christian parallel? Had they converted to Christianity and no one had ever told me?*

My mind was reeling! As I continued to read, I discovered that *Jesus* was not the *God of the Gentiles*, as I had always been told, but was in fact *Yeshua*, the Messiah of Israel. I nearly laughed out loud with joy as I learned that Yeshua was born to a Jewish mother in the Jewish homeland of Israel, and that all of His first followers were Jews.

And the Holy Spirit began to do a work inside of me, drawing me back to my own Jewish identity. Now if you think it was amazing when I opened the New Testament and discovered how Jewish it was, how much more of a shock do you think I experienced when I went back to my own Jewish Scriptures, the Scriptures that I supposedly believed in as a Jew and my parents believed in and the rabbi believed in? I began to read the Jewish Scriptures for myself as if for the very first time, and I discovered prophecy after prophecy that spoke about the Messiah. In almost every prophecy I saw Jesus!

I discovered that His name wasn't even Jesus, it was Yeshua. In Matthew it says His name would be called Yeshua, which means the "salvation of God" or "God saves," because He will save His people from their sins.

I realized that someone way back in history had spread a lie that said a Jew should not believe in Jesus. That the New Testament was not for Jews. That the Jewish Scriptures did not speak of Jesus as the Messiah. As I read hundreds of prophecies about Jesus in the Jewish Scriptures, I began to wonder, *Why don't the Jewish people see the truth?* The answer is that most have never read their own Scriptures.

One of my favorite prophecies is found in Jeremiah 31:31-34:

"The time is coming," declares the Lord, "when I will make a new covenant with the house of Israel and with the house of Judah."

This is a promise to all of the physical descendants of Abraham, Isaac, and Jacob even though they were split into the two tribes.

Verse 32: *"'It will not be like the covenant I made with their forefathers when I took them by the hand to lead them out of Egypt, because they broke My covenant, though I was a husband to them,' declares the Lord."*

When Jeremiah speaks of "the covenant...with their forefathers," he is clearly referring to the Mosaic covenant. Most Jewish people today still embrace the Mosaic covenant that's being spoken about here. But Jeremiah also prophesies a newer covenant that has not yet been accepted by the majority of the Jewish community.

God says in this Scripture that the reason for the new covenant is because *"they broke My covenant, though I was a husband to them."* So the Jewish people are being given this new covenant because they were unable to keep the old covenant. Rather than rejecting the Jewish people for breaking the previous covenant, He is offering them a new one. Do you see that? Now look at verse 33, *"'This is the covenant I will make with the house of Israel after that time,' declares the Lord."*

And then God mentions four things. One: *"I will put My law in their minds and write it on their hearts."* Number two: *"I will be their God, and they will be My people."* Number three:

"*No longer will they teach their neighbor, or say to one another, 'Know the Lord,' because they will all know Me....*" And number four: "*For I will forgive their wickedness and will remember their sins no more*" (v. 34).

These are four promises that God made in His new covenant. The first one tells us that the laws of God are going to be written on our hearts. The law has been taken off of tablets of stone and off of parchment and has been placed within our hearts by the Holy Spirit. Second, He will be our God and we will be His people. Third, we will all know God from the least to the greatest. This is not yet fulfilled. And then the fourth one, I will forgive their wickedness and remember their sins no more.

Only His blood can remove sin and remove all uncleanness from us. Animal sacrifice only covered our sin, but the Bible says that if we confess our sins, He is faithful and just to forgive us and to cleanse us from all unrighteousness through His own blood. So this is the new covenant. I remember staring in amazement at these words in our Jewish Scriptures written hundreds of years before Jesus was ever born.

I want you to catch one more thing. In verse 35 there's another prophecy that says, "*This is what the Lord says, He who appoints the sun to shine by day, who decrees the moon and stars to shine by night, who stirs up the sea so that its waves roar— the Lord Almighty is His name.*"

Now look at this: "*'Only if these decrees vanish from My sight,' declares the Lord, 'will the descendants of Israel ever cease to be a nation before Me'*" (v. 36).

> **Even though Israel rebelled, even though she was unfaithful, God is faithful. He made the covenant with Himself. God is being faithful to Himself to fulfill His promise to Israel.**

God is saying that as long as the sun is shining by day and the moon and the stars at night, He is going to preserve the Jewish people as a nation. Let's read on, "*Only if the heavens above can be measured and the foundations of the earth below be searched out will I reject all the descendants of Israel because of all they have done*" (v.37).

Even though Israel rebelled, even though she was unfaithful, God is faithful. He made the covenant with Himself. God is being faithful to Himself to fulfill His promise to Israel. And as long as there are stars and the moon at night and the sun during the day, as long as the heavens above haven't yet been measured, God will preserve the Jewish people.

Commentary by Sid Roth

Jonathan and I have been friends for more than 30 years. We have seen tens of thousands of Jewish people make peace with God through Messiah Jesus. I find it interesting that both of us had as a life goal to become a millionaire before age 30. We found something that money cannot buy. We found peace with God and peace within. As I write this commentary, His peace is bubbling throughout my entire body.

It's not like we are ostriches burying our heads in the sand. No! When God is for you, no one or thing can prosper who is against you.

We have no fear of sickness, poverty, or even death. It's the only way to really live.

CHAPTER 3
BY ROSE PRICE

CHAPTER 3

The Survivor

I am a survivor of Hitler's Holocaust. My family, who lived in a little city in Poland, was warm and caring. We looked out for one another. My relatives lived within walking distance of each other, so if it rained and you ducked into the nearest house, you were always in the home of a cousin or an aunt or uncle.

My upbringing was very Orthodox. My mother instilled in me that Judaism was life. I never knew a difference between a high holiday or a low holiday. A holiday was a holiday. Every *Shabbat* (Sabbath) was even celebrated as a holiday.

My mother and my grandmother would start getting ready for the Shabbat on Wednesday, baking *challa* (bread). On Friday they prepared the fish and the chicken soup and made the noodles. In the afternoon we would take a *cholent*—a one-pot dish with meat, vegetables, and potatoes—to the baker to cook.

We would take special baths and dress in our finest clothes. The table was all set in beautiful white linen and whatever silver we had.

Meal time was family time. On Friday nights we had fish. Father would come home from the synagogue and recite the *Kiddish*, the blessing over the wine and the *challa*; then he would bless the children.

Saturday morning we would go to the synagogue. After services, we would stop by the bakery and bring home the *cholent*. We all sat around grandmother's table and enjoyed the Sabbath meal.

The Nazi Horror

When Hitler took power, change came quickly. The Germans invaded in September 1939. One day at school shortly after the invasion, all the Jewish students were called up to the front of the classroom. With a guard standing nearby, our teacher told us, "Don't come back to the school anymore because you are Jews." I was ten and one-half years old. We were all absolutely devastated.

The next thing the Germans did was throw us out of our home and force us to live in a ghetto. They took the whole town of Jews and put us on one street.

My sister, who is two years older, and I were among the first to be sent away. We were on our way to visit our grandmother when the Germans grabbed us and put us to work in the ammunition factory.

It was a horror because we went from a warm house into freezing conditions, and from a loving, hugging, kissing family to a man constantly beating us with a whip. For a while we went back to our parents in the evenings. But one day, instead of letting us return home, they marched us into the woods. That summer I had been in the woods gathering mushrooms, blueberries, and raspberries. Now I was confined to a prison camp in those same woods.

> **That summer I had been in the woods gathering mushrooms, blueberries, and raspberries. Now I was confined to a prison camp in those same woods.**

It's unthinkable what those people did to us. It's almost indescribable. In the morning, they woke us up when it was still dark. We had to go outside, no matter what the weather was, and line up five deep for them to count us.

We worked a full day at the factory. I operated a machine that stretched out a piece of aluminum from a quarter of an inch to the length of a rifle bullet. I had to grease it, feed it, and take away the shells.

Before the invasion, my biggest responsibilities were to go to school, learn, come home, help my mother with the housework, do some gardening, and watch out for my younger sister. Now I was being told that either I learned how to work that machine or I would die. And I had to learn quickly.

I cried for a while, until one day I just couldn't cry anymore because I didn't have any tears left. That happened after the city was evacuated, and I knew I would never again see my parents or my family. That was my last day of crying for 25 years.

I prayed, and nothing happened.
When my prayers were not answered,
I concluded that there was no God.

At first I would still pray. I would get up in the morning and say the *Modeh Ani,* and during the day I would say the *Shema* and just pray to God. One day I prayed that God would send my mother because I was hungry and home-sick. I needed a mother's hug instead of the beatings. I wanted to take a bath because I was covered with dirt and we didn't have soap. I prayed, and nothing happened. When my prayers were not answered, I concluded that there was no God.

The Concentration Camps

I was transferred from one concentration camp to another until I was sent to Bergen-Belsen and then Dachau. It's hard for me to believe that I lived through such horror. Such horrible, horrible things happened at Bergen-Belsen. We were tortured. We were put in a field and forced to dig sugar beets out of the almost frozen ground with our bare hands. I remember my hands bleeding badly.

We had many difficult experiences in the camps. One stands out as particularly cruel. I was working in the field one day digging up sugar beets, and by then I was more like a zombie because I had been in these conditions for several years. I decided I was going to steal a sugar beet and eat it. I was determined that my belly was not going to hurt that night.

All we used to receive was a quarter-of-an-inch thick piece of bread—it was 80 percent sawdust—and a cup of coffee. That was our food for 24 hours. Obviously, this was barely enough food to exist on, let alone to sustain someone working in the extreme cold.

When the guard caught me, I got such a bad beating that even today when I talk about it I can still feel the cat-o'-nine tails on my back and on my face and around my body and the punishment of hanging by my hands—all because I stole a sugar beet.

**One time while we were lined up,
we were completely undressed for
an experiment to see how long it
would take for our blood to freeze.**

The cold weather alone killed many of us because we were not dressed properly. We would have to stand in line for hours, no matter how deep the snow was, half naked and without shoes.

One time while we were lined up, we were completely undressed for an experiment to see how long it would take for our blood to freeze. To this day, when I am in cold weather, and my toes and fingers go completely numb, I remember that time when my body started to freeze. The only reason I survived the experiment was because several people fell on top of me and their bodies kept me warm.

I had made up my mind that I would survive the same day that I had said there was no God. When I did survive, I took full credit. Later, I realized it had to have been the Lord.

But there were days when I thought I wasn't going to make it. When we were on our way to Dachau, our train was bombed. As we ran into the woods to get away from the train, I thought to myself, *That's it. I've made enough bullets. Let them use the bullets on me.* Death looked better than life.

One time when I was still in a camp in my own hometown, I was walking across the field with somebody, and I smiled. For the offense of smiling, the Germans put me in a sewer tank for 24 hours. I had to stay on my toes to keep from drowning. I was no more than 12 years old at the time.

> **For the offense of smiling,
> the Germans put me in a sewer
> tank for 24 hours. I had to stay on
> my toes to keep from drowning.**

Another difficult time was when my sister, who was in the same camp, got typhoid fever. She was my last living family member, and I didn't think I could go on if I lost her too. The guards came in periodically to check for those who were sick. Then they would take them outside and leave them to freeze. I laid on top of my sister to protect her, and when they asked for people to lift up their hands to show they were healthy, I put my hand up in place of hers.

Selected to Be Shot

Twice, I was selected to be shot. Both times when the guards unlocked the chain, I ran away. The second time I ran into a guard. I was running so hard I bounced off of him. But he didn't see me. It could only have been God. If he had seen me, he would have shot me himself. I looked up at him and then fled into a wooded part of the camp.

When we were finally liberated in May 1945, I was full of unforgiveness for what I had been through. I hated the Germans with a passion. The unforgiveness literally poisoned my body, causing me to need 27 operations.

I was looking for somebody who would be willing to drop a bomb on Germany and Poland. I had lost all of my family except my sister and one aunt—nearly 100 relatives.

My New Life

After I was released, I came to America, got married, and had children. As much as I hated God, I became active in the traditional synagogue. My children needed to learn about Judaism, but I couldn't teach them because I was dead inside. Socially, I was the best Jew. I was active in helping to build the Hebrew school. I even worked my way up to become president of the sisterhood.

If someone had asked me back then, "Do you believe in God?" I would have said, "No." Even today many rabbis don't believe in the Bible, and very few believe in God. But I believed in maintaining my Jewish identity and tradition.

My Daughter Believes in Jesus

One day my teenage daughter came to me and said the worst thing I could imagine. She said, "Mommy, I believe in Jesus Christ, and He is the Jewish Messiah." I nearly had a heart attack. I told her what Jesus Christ did to her family and why she didn't have many aunts and uncles. The Nazi guards had told me over and over that because I killed Jesus Christ, He hated me and put me into the camps to kill me.

> **She said, "Mommy, I believe in Jesus Christ, and He is the Jewish Messiah."**

When I was seven or eight years old, I was hit in the head with a crucifix by a priest in Poland for the "crime" of walking on the sidewalk in front of his church.

So for my daughter to believe in Jesus Christ was death. I threw her out. I couldn't have this enemy living in my house. When my husband went to the house where she was staying to check on her, he became a believer too. The house was used as an outreach to Jewish people.

My younger daughter was still going to a private Hebrew school. But somehow I knew that she had secretly become a Messianic believer, and I beat her for it, even though I don't remember doing it.

> **I had lost my first family under Hitler, and now was about to lose my second family, all because of this Jesus. I was ready to meet Jesus and kill Him.**

After my husband accepted the Lord, he came home and started reading Proverbs 31 to me. I didn't know what Proverbs 31 was, but when he told me he believed also, he became a traitor to me too. The rabbi couldn't do anything with him. He was very stubborn. I was ready to leave my family, but I couldn't. A friend of mine, a lawyer, said, "If you leave the house, the authorities will put you in jail for desertion of your minor children."

I had lost my first family under Hitler, and now was about to lose my second family, all because of this Jesus. I was ready to meet Jesus and kill Him.

I tried everything possible to reach both children. For the first time I told them about the concentration camps. I begged them. I pleaded with them to reject this Jewish enemy. For two thousand years we had been persecuted because this man was supposed to be a Messiah. I told them everything I had learned, and nothing helped.

Since my husband had become a believer, he insisted that my daughter come back home. They witnessed to me constantly. I would find my Jewish Bible opened and little pieces of paper with Scriptures on it.

I didn't know they were Scriptures because I didn't know the Bible.

I Go to the Rabbi

I ran to the rabbi. He would tell me different Scriptures with which to challenge my family. In response, they would give me five more.

At the urging of my family, I asked the rabbi about Isaiah 53. He said, "No Jew reads that, especially a Jewish woman." So I couldn't read it. The same with Psalm 22. There are 328 prophecies of the coming of the suffering servant Messiah. I asked the rabbi about almost all of them. Finally, the rabbi told me not to come to the synagogue anymore because I had read him Isaiah 53.

I kept yelling and screaming and crying, "Help me! I'm not going that way. What do you want from me? My family is dead because they believe in Jesus, you tell me, but my food disappears. Who is eating the food? Why do I have so much laundry? If they are all dead, then why is it? Help me!"

> **I started sneaking down to the basement and reading the New Testament in a locked room.**

He just replied, "No. I can't help you anymore."

So I started sneaking down to the basement and reading the New Testament in a locked room. I read Matthew first, and it showed me Jesus was a gentle man. He wasn't a killer of my people, but a very gentle man. Then I started to think about what I believed.

I went to another rabbi for help, but he said, "Look, I can't help you because I don't read the Bible very much."

The Millionaire

Shortly after that encounter I went to a dinner at Arthur DeMoss' house. Mr. DeMoss was a wealthy Christian businessman who would open his home once a year as an outreach to Jewish people. He asked me if I would mind if he prayed for me. I told him, "I don't care if you stand on your head. It's your house." Instead of standing on his head, he started to pray. Jews never close their eyes in prayer, but all of a sudden I closed my eyes and said a very simple prayer:

> God of Abraham, Isaac, and Jacob, if it's true, if He who they are saying is Your Son, and You have a Son, and He is really the Messiah, OK. But, Father, if He isn't, forget that I talked to You.

That was the first prayer I had prayed since 1942. I felt the biggest stone rolling off my back. For the first time since the war, I cried, and I felt so clean. I knew He was real, and I made Him *my* Messiah.

> **For the first time since the war, I
> cried, and I felt so clean. I knew He
> was real, and I made Him *my* Messiah.**

When Holocaust survivors get angry with me today because I am a Messianic Jew, I just show love to them because I know how they feel. I've been there. I don't argue with them.

Berlin Calls

One day I got a call from Sid Roth. A friend of his, a pastor from a large church in Berlin, had just called him to say, "We're going to rent the largest coliseum in Berlin, the one that Hitler used for his meetings, and we're looking for Messianic Jews to take part in the events we have planned."

Sid said, "I have the perfect person," meaning me. But when he called me, I refused.

When I left Germany I swore I would never, ever go back to that accursed land. And here he was asking me to go back to Germany. *How could he?* For six months I wrestled about whether to go. I asked the Lord to kill me, to take me home, but not to send me back because as soon as I started praying, the word came, "Yes, you have to go back, and you have to forgive."

I finally surrendered. I went with my husband and four other believers. Many more came later. It was, as I said, a six-month struggle. I had people pray and fast for me.

This was a big event. A number of prominent Christians were there including Pat Robertson, Demos Shakarian, and Pat Boone.

When I walked into that coliseum, the one where Hitler said the Nazis would rule the world for a thousand years, it was jam packed with young Germans. A number of them had stars of David, Jewish stars, around their necks. Israeli flags were waving.

When I saw the American leaders, some of whom I knew, and I saw the German people wearing stars of David and mezuzahs, I thought, *It's impossible.* Then I thought, *What am I doing here? Lord, what do you want from me? Get me out of here. I don't want to speak German. Am I doing this right, or am I telling the Germans and the world that it's OK to go kill Jews?* These thoughts tormented me until I spoke.

Confronted by Nazis

On Sunday they called me up to speak. I don't remember saying the things that were printed. I don't remember speaking on forgiveness. But after I finished my talk, some people came up to me who were the last people on the face of this earth that I wanted to see. They were ex-Nazis. Apparently, I had asked for any ex-Nazis to come up and be prayed for and forgiven. I don't remember saying it, but here they were asking me to forgive them. Could I forgive them face-to-face as I had from the podium?

That's when I realized that I had spoken on forgiveness. One of those who had come forward was a guard from

Dachau. He had been in charge of punishment. When he came and identified himself, my body shriveled up in pain as he knelt down. He was pleading with me to forgive him.

I am a believer, but people cannot comprehend what I experienced in Dachau and Bergen-Belsen. They cannot imagine the hell I went through. It was only by the grace of God that I was able to forgive those who came forward, because Rose Price could not forgive them for the atrocities I went through as a child.

> ...one of the ex-Nazis whom I had prayed with for forgiveness came up to me. He said that after I had prayed with him he had his first night's sleep since the war.

As I was ready to leave Berlin, one of the ex-Nazis whom I had prayed with for forgiveness came up to me. He said that after I had prayed with him he had his first night's sleep since the war.

Show Me the Strength

Another time I was in Germany again, and I realized I was not far from Bergen-Belsen. I knew that I had to go back. Once and for all I had to bury Bergen-Belsen. I had a Swedish couple with me, Susan and Gary, and a German man named Otto—all believers.

I had to ask a guide for the location of the main gate. I didn't recognize it because the barracks had all been burned. But I knew if they put me where the main gate had been, I could find where the barracks had stood. I was amazed that even today no grass grows where the electric wires were located. No matter how many times they plant grass, it does not grow. The guide gave me a list of the names of those who had been at Bergen-Belsen, and I found my sister's and my name on the list. We were on the last transport out from Bergen-Belsen to Dachau. After that, all those who remained died of typhus.

I cried, and I wept. At one point I was hollering at Bergen-Belsen, "You died, but I survived! I am here! I survived!"

While I was hollering, I started to pray for the salvation of the country and that the German people would learn of the Messiah's love and forgiveness.

At one point I asked, "Lord, how can I pray that prayer at this cemetery where so much happened to me, so much that is indescribable?"

As I was praying, the German man became hysterical. I went over to him to hug him, and he said, "How can you pray for us when we did that to you? My family was involved with this. We put you here. How can you? Show me the strength. Show me the strength." Then he asked for forgiveness, and the four of us just kept on crying and praying for one another and for the German people.

You Have to Forgive

If you feel you cannot forgive someone, you cannot hate anyone more than I hated the Germans. I lost my stomach. I had 27 operations before I went to Berlin. Hate has an address in your body. Love cannot dwell in the body with hate. When I finally gave up all the hate and love started coming in, something happened inside my body. I didn't have pain anymore. I haven't had an operation since 1981 because the Lord has taken all that poison out of me.

> **Nobody knows the pain you have gone through, and nobody knows the pain I went through. But there is no excuse for hate. You have to forgive.**

Nobody knows the pain you have gone through, and nobody knows the pain I went through. But there is no excuse for hate. You have to forgive. You have to give up the hate.

It's not even up to you to have the strength to forgive. You cannot do anything in your own power. You have to go to the Lord, and the Lord will give you the strength.

Commentary by Sid Roth

What kind of power could allow Rose Price to forgive Nazis who tortured and murdered almost her entire family?

This power is the Holy Spirit of God. God predicts a day will come in which He will change man's heart and give him a new spirit: "I will give you a new heart, and a new spirit will I put within you;

and I will remove the heart of stone out of your body..." (Ezek. 36:26).

This new Spirit that God will put within us will allow us to live at a higher level and overcome all fears. Jeremiah 31:30,33 (31,34 in some versions), written hundreds of years before the birth of Jesus, predicts a new covenant from God that will not only cause God to remember our sins no more, but allow us to *know* Him!

Imagine having intimacy with God. You can hear His voice. You can experience His love. I know this is true because I know Him. And what He has done for me, He desires to do for you.

CHAPTER 4
BY ALYOSHA RYABINOV

CHAPTER 4

A New Song

I was born to Jewish parents in Kiev in 1958. My parents tried to hide our Jewishness. There was nothing Jewish in our home, and we never attended synagogue. Yet even as a child, I wanted to be Jewish because my mother and father were. I couldn't rationalize it, but it just felt right inside.

As I grew up, the only religion I was exposed to was atheism. Atheism was taught in the former Soviet Union as the truth. In college they even offered a course on it in which they ridiculed people who believed in God. When my professor claimed that science had proven one hundred times over that there is no God, I wanted to ask for even one proof out of a hundred. I didn't feel atheism was based on any scientific proof. But I didn't have the courage to voice my inner thoughts.

I Knew There Was a God

I somehow knew there was a God. I knew that even something as simple as a wristwatch could never have been constructed through random acts of chance. How could all those tiny pieces of metal have assembled themselves together over millions of years? Only a fool would believe that.

If a wristwatch could not have evolved, how could they ever expect me to believe that something as complicated as a human being just "happened"? Even one cell in the human body is much more complex than a watch. People have to be blind to deny the existence of a Creator.

I come from a family of musicians. My grandfather was a violinist and composer. My father was a violinist. My mother is a classical guitarist. They were well known in the former Soviet Union. My father even played in the orchestra, which was a great accomplishment since Jews were discriminated against. When I was five years old, I began to study piano at music school. I didn't know how good I was until I entered a few competitions in the fifth and sixth grades. To my surprise, I won the first prize twice. After I finished music school and decided I was going to be a professional musician, I practiced between six and eight hours a day at least six days a week.

I appeared to be on my way to a promising career, except for one thing—I was Jewish. In the Soviet Union, that was a major drawback. When a Jewish person wanted to enter college or pursue a career, it was much harder for him simply because he was Jewish. In spite of the odds, I did manage to gain admission to college and earn my bachelor's degree.

The next step for me would have been to attend the conservatory. I was talented enough to get in, but at that time my grandfather emigrated to the United States. This was in 1979 before large numbers were allowed to leave. Now I had two strikes against me: I was Jewish and the grandson of a "traitor." My grandfather was a well-known art critic. Because the circles of music and art are so closely aligned, everyone in music knew that my grandfather now lived in a capitalist country. As a result, they would never accept me into the conservatory.

The Long Wait

At that point, I wanted to get out of the country so badly I didn't care where I went. Of course, the authorities made the process very difficult. I don't know of one person during that time who was allowed to emigrate without great challenges. You are required to gather numerous documents, some of which are ridiculous. For example, a friend of mine who was divorced for many years had to get a document from his former wife saying that she would allow him to leave.

In the office where I submitted the documents, they called me a traitor. I was prepared for the verbal abuse, but it wasn't pleasant. I didn't feel I had betrayed my country. I believed every person should have a choice where to live.

After I turned in all the documents, I had to wait. Some people were forced to wait for years. Eventually, someone calls you and tells you whether you can go or not. But the waiting period is very difficult. I couldn't work because I had applied for permission to emigrate and no one would hire me. And now the army wanted to draft me. They do that to bring more fear and harassment.

When I had waited for about eight months, I started to get very anxious. I learned that in some cases people were denied permission to emigrate. I became very fearful. I thought, *What if they don't let me leave? If that happens I can never establish myself as a musician in Russia.* I would always be persecuted. People would always know that I had tried to "escape" from Russia, and my future life would be full of misery.

> I needed to pour out my heart to someone, but I didn't feel there was any human who could possibly help me. So I thought, if there were a God in Heaven, I should try Him.

I needed to pour out my heart to someone, but I didn't feel there was any human who could possibly help me. So I thought, if there were a God in Heaven, I should try Him. The question was, Where do I find Him? My first instinct was to go to a synagogue, but I didn't know where any were. And you don't want to walk around the streets of the Soviet

Union asking, "Where's the nearest synagogue?" If the person you talk to is KGB, you might end up in prison.

So I decided to go to a church instead. The one I found happened to be Russian Orthodox. As I walked inside, I got confused by all the pictures of saints on the walls. There were so many, I didn't know which one to pray to. As I walked around the church, I saw a replica of Jesus (Yeshua is His Hebrew name) on the cross. My atheism class helped me because I had learned that Jesus is for the Christians. Of course they taught that He never existed, even as a man. I certainly didn't know anything about all the saints pictured there. So I decided to pray to Jesus. I said, "Jesus, please get me out of this country." Then I turned around and left.

Our family received permission to emigrate soon after that. But I forgot about the prayer. We emigrated in 1979 to Chicago. Right away I started to study music at DePaul University.

Now that I was in a free country, I wanted to investigate my Jewish roots. I began to read about Jewish history. I even went to a reformed synagogue a few times. Although I was a bit bored with the service, I was excited to be among my people. My heritage had been withheld from me for so long, it was like getting back something that had been stolen. I also got involved at a Jewish community center.

I Find the Messiah

One thing I learned was that Christians and Jews do not mix. I never knew that before. My atheism course had taught me a little about different religions, but I didn't know that Jews were told not to accept Jesus as their Messiah.

> **One day my sister came home and told our mother she believed in God and that Jesus was the Jewish Messiah. Mom didn't take it very well.**

One day my sister came home and told our mother she believed in God and that Jesus was the Jewish Messiah. Mom didn't take it very well. As they discussed the matter, I listened from another room. To my surprise, what my sister said made sense to me. That was a miracle in itself, because I never gave much weight to anything she had to say.

Quietly, without telling anyone, I began to read books about Jesus that my sister had brought home. One book was about several rabbis who had found the Messiah. That was stunning to me. I was totally amazed that a rabbi could believe in Jesus. The book also discussed prophecies of the Bible that had been fulfilled. I was fascinated by passages such as Isaiah 53, which contained so many Messianic prophecies.

I wanted to know the truth. So I asked God to give me a sign if Jesus really was the Messiah. Suddenly, a bright light came into my room. It stayed for a little while, and then it left. But even after God had answered my prayer for emigration to the U.S. and now had sent this supernatural light, I was still not willing to admit to anyone what I was beginning to believe. I had grown up in such unbelief that I asked God for another sign, but I didn't get any more.

My sister attended Bible studies with a group that met right in the midst of the Jewish community. My mother feared that my sister would be persecuted for believing in Jesus and asked her not to go back. But my sister said, "I really want to study the Bible. Can the group come to our house?" Since our house was not close to the Jewish community center, my mother agreed. When the group arrived for their meeting, they invited me to join them. I wanted to, but I still didn't want to admit it. I said, "I'm not interested, but I'll sit and listen." During the course of the Bible study, the leader suddenly pointed to me and asked, "Do you believe that Yeshua is the Messiah?" Immediately, I was going to respond, "No," but I couldn't. Instead, a new-found strength welled up within me, and I said, "Yes." By the time I told my mother, she had grown more accustomed to the idea. It didn't matter that much to her whether we believed in Jesus or not. She was just afraid of persecution from the traditional Jewish community.

> **By the time I told my mother, she had grown more accustomed to the idea. It didn't matter that much to her whether we believed in Jesus or not. She was just afraid of persecution from the traditional Jewish community.**

When I finished my master's degree program at DePaul University, I gave two recitals. They were the best achievements of my life. For the two hours that I played the concerts and for a short time afterward, I felt a great sense of accomplishment. People really loved the performances and praised me. But by the following day, I felt empty. All those hours of daily practice year after year had yielded only a couple brief moments of glory. Now the glory was gone, and all that was left was this strange, empty feeling. At first, I wanted to produce and play more great music so people would lift me up again and tell me I was wonderful. Otherwise, I felt I would sink. It's natural to desire to be great, but we are not to use it to bring glory to ourselves. The Lord showed me He wanted me to live my whole life for Him. So for a year I didn't play piano. And for about two years, I didn't give any significant concerts. Piano was an idol for me. I put my idol on the altar and said, "If you don't want me to use this for the rest of my life, I won't. I want my life to magnify You, God."

In the meantime, I attended Moody Bible Institute, where I met my wife, Jody, who also is Jewish and believes in Yeshua. After one semester, we had an opportunity to go to Israel. A highlight of my time there was when I prayed for a boy with epilepsy. Jody and I went to see him with a Russian friend who had just become a believer in Jesus. It was difficult to communicate because we didn't share a common language. We spoke English and Russian and the boy's mother spoke Spanish and Hebrew. God showed me there was a demon causing the epilepsy. So for the first time in my life I told a demon to get out in the name of Jesus.

Suddenly, the boy indicated he felt something leave him. He did not know what I had prayed because he didn't understand the language. Months later I found out that he never had any more occurrences of epilepsy!

> **God showed me there was a demon causing the epilepsy. ...I told a demon to get out in the name of Jesus. Suddenly, the boy indicated he felt something leave him.**

Playing for God

After we returned from Israel, I began to understand that I was to use my talent for the piano to serve God. I also felt the desire to praise God with singing. That was interesting to me because I don't sing very well. Anyone who becomes a new believer can receive a new song, whether he is a musician or not. When that new song started to come out of me, I went to the piano and began to praise God. Some beautiful new music compositions came out of it.

God has continued in His faithfulness to me over the years. He has given me the opportunity to play in Sweden, Germany, Austria, Ukraine, Israel, and Canada, as well as the United States. I now have eight music recordings. And God has blessed Jody and me with two wonderful children, Josiah and Yasmine. Maybe you are experiencing great difficulties in your life as I did. I looked in many different directions for the answers. But I found that the only way to have true peace and victory is through knowing the Messiah. He will put a new song in your mouth.

Commentary by Sid Roth

Although most American Jews are agnostics, most Russian Jews are taught to be atheists. This is rapidly changing in both countries. Hundreds of thousands of Russian Jews like Alyosha are now believers in Jesus. And there are hundreds of Messianic Jewish synagogues in America to accommodate Jewish believers in Jesus.

Where do you stand? Do you believe there is a God who created the world? When I was in school, the theory of evolution sounded reasonable. Today, I realize it takes more faith to believe this complex universe evolved through chance than to believe the account of creation in the Bible.

Consider the example Alyosha gave of a wristwatch. If you took it completely apart and shook the pieces around in a box for a million years, would it come out reassembled and ticking? How much more complex is the heart and the thousands of miles of capillaries that help make up the circulatory system!

Did you know the human eye has one million nerve fibers in each optic nerve? Each one is connected to the brain. When the eye points at something, it sends a message to the brain that tells the brain the distance to the object. The brain then sends a message to the muscles of the lens telling it how much to change its curvature. In a split second, the object is in focus.

In the last 24 hours your heart has beat 100,000 times; your blood has traveled 186 million miles throughout 60,000 miles of tubing in your body. Your kidneys have filtered over 42 gallons of liquid. And you have probably exercised 7 million brain cells. No machine made by man compares with your body.

By the way, if man evolved from the monkey, why have we never found full fossils or animals that are part ape and part human? And why has *every* "missing link" between apes and men turned out to be a mistake or hoax?

I remember in high school we used to study the evolutionary date charts. They stated as fact that dinosaurs lived millions of years *before man*. At the Creation Evidences Museum in Glynn Rose, Texas, we can see evidence of *human and dinosaur footprints made within minutes of each other* captured in a limestone bed. Actually, this same limestone has 57 human footprints and 192 dinosaur prints—proof the evolutionary charts are fantasy. Man and dinosaurs lived on Earth together.

What about the "Big Bang" theory? If a big explosion created order out of chaos, why has every observable explosion in history brought disorder? The Bible says the real "big bang" is yet to come:

> *But the day of the Lord will come as a thief in the night, in which the heavens will pass away with a great noise, and the elements will melt with fervent heat; both the earth and the works that are in it will be burned up* (2 Peter 3:10 NKJV).

Then God will bring us a new heaven and a new earth. It will be in perfect order—a garden of Eden:

> *Now I saw a new heaven and a new earth, for the first heaven and the first earth had passed away* ... (Revelation 21:1 NKJV).

CHAPTER 5
BY SHARON R. ALLEN

CHAPTER 5

Yiddishkeit

My life in 1982 was dedicated to the well-being of my family and to my activities at Chabad of Irvine Jewish Center. One can find Chabad centers in even the most remote communities of the world. I have always had a deep admiration for Chabad, and that is why my husband and I supported the Chabad movement here in Southern California.

But wait, I'm getting ahead of myself. I want to go back to the beginning—my beginning.

I was born in 1945 at Beth Israel Hospital in New York City. My Hebrew name is Sura Rifka. I was raised in an observant Jewish home. From the moment my mom lit the *Shabbos* (Sabbath) candles on Friday evening until one hour after sundown on Saturday night, there were certain rules and regulations that we followed. They did not make us feel constricted or oppressed. It was our way of showing our love, our respect, and our devotion to God.

We followed the rabbinical injunctions, such as not using electricity on the Shabbos. We would leave one light on in the hall which was turned on before Shabbos started and was left on through the night and the next day until one hour after sundown Saturday night when Shabbos was over. We were not permitted to work on Shabbos, and that included my homework, since on Shabbos one is not allowed to write on, cut, or tear paper. We knew that the Shabbos was special because of what we did or did not do, and it was distinct from the other days of the week.

Of course, my mother kept a kosher kitchen where only kosher foods were permitted. Separate sets of dishes and utensils designated for *milchig* (dairy) or *fleishig* (meat) products were strictly enforced. My brother and I knew from the time we could reach up into the drawers and cabinets never to confuse those items deemed milchig and fleishig. Separate sets of dishes were also needed for Passover. Those dishes were brought out of the "hard-to-reach" top cabinet once a year to be used only on Pesach.

We observed all the Jewish holidays. My brother and I attended Hebrew School. We grew up knowing who we were within the Jewish Community.

Moving West

As a young adult, I married a man from a similar Jewish background. We had a daughter, whom we named Elisa.

Her Hebrew name is Chava Leah. When she was only a few years old, we divorced. We received a Jewish divorce, known as a *get*.

I worked in the "Garment Center" in New York City. During this time Elisa attended Jewish Day School. I remember those early years when Elisa and I would wait for her school bus on cold, snowy, dark winter mornings at seven o'clock. We would huddle together freezing in the wind. It was on such a morning when I whispered to my daughter, "There has got to be a better way."

Moving out of state seemed like a step in the right direction. Elisa had an allergy problem that was worse during the damp winter months. New York had the worst winter climate for children like her. I had heard a doctor on a talk show mention that when people with certain allergies moved to another climate, their allergies would often disappear. With that doctor's words echoing in my ears, I sat down and made a list of the leading Garment Centers in the country. The doctor's theory about the benefits of moving was certainly worth a try.

On August 27, 1974, Elisa and I arrived in Los Angeles, California. Almost immediately, I enrolled her in Yavneh Yeshiva because school was starting in September. She was six years old. We lived near the school in the Fairfax District, the Orthodox section of town, and became involved with the Shaari Tefillah Congregation.

In a few years, my parents moved to Los Angeles to join us, and shortly after that we moved south to Orange County. At that time there was a big real estate boom, and, like many others, I decided to get my real estate license. Once I received my license, I started to work in an office owned by a man named Ron Allen. He was to become my husband.

Business Was His Religion

When Ron and I first met, he knew I was Jewish and that I was raised in an observant Jewish home. All I knew about Ron's religious background was that he was a Protestant. He never mentioned Jesus, the New Testament, or church. If he had, I would have run in the opposite direction. Apparently, he hadn't been to church since he was a teenager. He was 42. I was 32. Religion was the furthest thing from Ron's mind; business was his religion.

As Ron got to know our Jewish traditions, he embraced them as his own and eagerly participated. Because of Ron's warm and loving ways, my parents welcomed him into the family. My mother would say about Ron, "He's so *hamisha*," which in Yiddish means, "He's so comfortable to be with."

We were active in Chabad and became attached to the rabbi, Mendel Duchman, whom we admired and respected. Part scholar, part showman, and part businessman, Rabbi Duchman was successful in renewing peoples' interest in the Jewish lifestyle. His wife Rochel was warm, caring, and knowledgeable. She was the picture of the young, Jewish *balaboosta* (conscientious, immaculate housewife), a *rebbetzen's rebbetzen* (rabbi's wife), so to speak.

Ron and I knew right away that this was where we belonged. I became very active in the Chabad women's group.

Converting to Judaism

A few years after Ron and I were married, our discussions about his converting to Judaism turned serious. I knew that our future together could be impaired if Ron refused. Having a Jewish home and raising Elisa Jewish was foremost in my mind. In order to be a successful Jew, you must ask yourself the question: "Are your grandchildren Jewish?" and be able to answer in the affirmative. When Ron legally adopted Elisa shortly after our marriage, even the adoption papers stipulated that Elisa would be raised Jewish.

> **...consideration of burial
> and the afterlife for a
> Jew are of vital importance.**

In addition, consideration of burial and the afterlife for a Jew are of vital importance. As a Jew, I knew that burial in a Jewish cemetery was a must. We believe that if we are buried in a Jewish cemetery, we will roll underground all the way to Eretz Yisroel and be among the first to be resurrected. As Jews, we believe that we go to Paradise or Abraham's Bosom. If we should accidentally wander to the "other place," Father Abraham "pulls us back."

The importance for me of being an observant Jew is underscored by the following story from the Talmud (Tractate Berachot 28b) about Rabbi Yochanon Ben Zakkai on his deathbed. The rabbi's students were shocked to find their master weeping. Asked to explain his behavior, the sage responded that if he were being taken before a king of flesh and blood whose punishment was *not eternal* and who could be bribed and appeased, he would still be deathly afraid; imagine how he must feel as he finds himself coming before the King of Kings, *who lives forever, whose punishment is eternal and who can neither be bribed nor appeased.* Moreover, two roads lay before him, the sage explained, one led to Heaven and one to hell, and with such prospects, should he not be afraid?

In the January 1989 issue of the *B'nai B'rith Messenger,* "Torah Thoughts," the Rebbe Menachem M. Schneerson writes about this story:

> The Talmud relates that when the great sage Rabbi Yochanon Ben Zakkai wept before his death, he said: 'There are two paths stretching before me, one to Gan Eden [heaven] and one to Gehinom; I know not on which I shall be led.' It goes without saying that Rabbi Yochanon Ben Zakkai was concerned with his spiritual status and if he had attained a sufficient level of holiness to enter heaven.
>
> These concerns are from a man who is credited with the survival of Diaspora Judaism and whose influence has been felt throughout the ages. Rabbi Yochanon Ben Zakkai leaves behind him the expansion of Jewish thought and law, Babylonian Talmud, Responsa literature, Rishonim, Achronim, Chassidut, and Mussar. *But he didn't know for sure whether he was going to Heaven or hell.*

Is it any wonder this story got my attention? If such an eminent and renowned Torah scholar as Rabbi Yochanon Ben Zakkai is uncertain where he is bound, it is incumbent upon us to do whatever is necessary to ensure our future fate and to be deemed worthy of Gan Eden.

Another important consideration regarding Ron's conversion had to do with the Israeli Rabbinate who accept only Orthodox conversions. So we knew that only a kosher conversion would do.

As part of any Jewish conversion, the study of Jewish life, history, and ethics is vital. Ron was exposed to *Yiddishkeit* (Jewish lifestyle) in our home. I looked forward to his education with Rabbi Duchman.

> **As part of any Jewish conversion, the study of Jewish life, history, and ethics is vital.**

Before this conversion was to take place, I wanted to make Ron aware of the three ceremonies that would be required. I explained that males needed to be circumcised, and that since he was already circumcised, the rabbi would draw a bit of blood from the penis as a symbolic gesture. It would also be necessary for him to be immersed in water in a *mikvah*. This is similar to baptism and symbolizes purification and identification with the Jewish people. The third ceremony, though not always done in Reformed or Conservative conversions, must always accompany an Orthodox or "kosher" conversion, and that is the renouncing of a person's prior beliefs before a *Beit Din* or rabbinical court (council of rabbis).

It's So Pagan!

Ron agreed to all the ceremonies but the last one. He said he just didn't think he could renounce Jesus.

I was horrified!

My husband had never mentioned Jesus, hadn't been to church for more than 30 years, and had never used the words "Christian," "Christ," or "New Testament." Here we were leading a Jewish life—we helped to build the synagogue, our home was used by the Jewish community, our daughter was attending Hebrew Academy—*and my husband was telling me he couldn't renounce Jesus!*

> **Ron agreed to all the ceremonies but the last one. He said he just didn't think he could renounce Jesus.**

I was so upset. I said to my husband, "This is crazy. You're such a smart and logical person and such a successful businessman. How can you believe in something so pagan? It's a fantasy. It's like Greek mythology!"

And then in the midst of my horror came this calming thought—I'll just begin to read the Jewish Bible, and in no time at all I will be able to show my husband the Scriptures that will prove to him that Jesus could never have been the fulfillment of the Jewish Bible. I knew that everything God wanted His Jewish people to know about His Jewish Messiah, so that we Jews would recognize Him when He would come, would be in my Jewish Bible.

Is Jesus in the Jewish Bible?

I marched downstairs to the family room and took my Jewish Bible off the shelf. As I opened it that day, I prayed a very specific prayer. I prayed to the God of Abraham, Isaac, and Jacob to show me the truth and to help my husband become a Jew.

That morning as my husband went to work and my daughter to school, I began to read my Bible. I started at page one, "In the beginning," and continued to read page after page. When my husband came home from work and my daughter from school, there I was still reading. The next morning, when my husband went to work and my daughter to school, there I was reading. When they came home again, there I was still reading. This went on for days, for weeks, and then months. I was amazed at what I found written within the pages of my Jewish Bible.

> **I was amazed at what I found written within the pages of my Jewish Bible.**

You see, every Jew feels that he basically knows what's in his own Jewish Bible. That's because as children we attend

Hebrew School, Yeshiva, or Cheder; then as adults, we attend synagogue where we hear a portion read from the Torah and a portion from the *Haftorah* (the Prophets).

Within the pages of my Jewish Bible, there is much written concerning the Messiah—where He would be born, how He would live His life, the miracles He would do. The Bible also speaks of His suffering and death. It frightened me because what I read sounded very much like what I heard said about Jesus. Whoever may be wondering if Yeshua (Jesus) appears in the Jewish Bible need only read the many passages concerning the *Malach Ha Shem*, The Messenger of the Lord. By carefully studying the passages concerning His appearances and how He conducts Himself, one can only deduce that this is no mere created being. He speaks as God and accepts the worship that can *only* be given to God Himself. And He carries in Him the ineffable name of God, the Tetragrammaton, in Hebrew, the *Yud Hay Vav Hay* (see Exod. 23:21).

In addition, *Yeshua*, Jesus' Hebrew name, means "salvation." Everywhere in the Jewish Bible and our Jewish Holy Prayer books, whenever the word "salvation" appears, we are saying Jesus' Hebrew name, Yeshua.

In Proverbs 30:4 I found that God has a Son...

In Isaiah 49:6, the Scriptures speak of a time when the Suffering Servant would lament to God of how He had failed to restore the 12 tribes of Israel. God responds by saying, "It's too light a thing for You to be a servant for Israel only, I will give You as a light to all the nations of the world." In Hebrew the word translated "nations" is *goyim*. So I had to ask myself the question, When did the Messiah come and fail to bring back the tribes of Israel, and then when did God give the Messiah to the goyim?

God Had a Son?

I learned that the ancient Jewish writers recognized that there are two pictures of the Messiah depicted in the pages of the Jewish Bible. They even had names for them: *Moshiach Ben Yoseph* (Messiah, son of Joseph)—the suffering servant Messiah, and *Moshiach Ben Dovid* (Messiah, son of David)—the Messiah who would come as the conquering hero.

In Proverbs 30:4 I found that God has a Son:

> *Who was it that ascended into heaven, and came down again? who gathered the wind in his fists? who bound the waters in a garment? who set up all the ends of the earth? what is his name, and what is his son's name, if thou knowest it?*

Could the Rebbe Be the Messiah?

When I finished reading all the pages of my Jewish Bible, I was confused and frightened. The thought came to me, *Sharon, how dare you think that you could interpret the Bible by yourself, as if you knew as much as a rabbi.* But then I would think about the passages I read where God told the children of Israel to come and hear His Word for themselves (see Deut. 4:10,29; 11:18-20; and Jer. 29:13).

I knew I couldn't stop there. There was too much at stake.

How could I even bear the thought of being an outcast from my people? How absurd it was to think that a man the Gentiles call Jesus Christ could be a Messiah for the Jews. So I said to myself, "Sharon, you must have missed something!"

I remembered that the rabbis say, "You cannot understand the Bible without the Jewish Commentaries." So I bought the Rashi commentaries, the Soncino commentaries, and the latest Jewish commentaries called *The ArtScroll Tanach Series* by Mesorah Publications. And as I read the commentaries, the more I wanted to read. I also brought home texts from the *Babylonian Talmud*, the *Encyclopedia Judaica*, *Midrash Rabbah*, *Mishneh Torah* by Maimonides, *Targum Onkelos*, *Targumim Jonathan*, *The Messiah Texts* by Raphael Patai, and the *Guide to the Perplexed* by Maimonides. On and on I studied, day after day. With each text I studied, I thought maybe this one will hold the answer, the key to destroying the thought that this *goyishe* messiah is the "real thing"—*the Jewish Messiah!*

All this was beginning to affect my life. When asked if I would accept a role in the leadership as next president of Chabad Women, I felt I had to decline because I was leading a double existence.

I was fully accepted by Chabad and adhered to all the traditions. I even went to a cable television station periodically to hear the Rebbe Menachem M. Schneerson speak to his followers via satellite. I held this man in high esteem. He was respected and consulted by leaders of the world. All of us who listened to him believed that he spoke the truth. It always seemed in those days it could very well be true that one day it would be revealed that the Rebbe Menachem M. Schneerson was the Messiah. It is a popular belief among Chabad followers that in each generation the Messiah dwells among us, but if we are not worthy, he will not be revealed to us. So here I was listening to this Jewish leader believing that he spoke the truth, and yet, at the same time, I was researching ancient Jewish material to find the truth about Jesus! During the next few months, my home library increased. And my fears multiplied proportionately to the number of books I accumulated.

Not to Worry

One afternoon Elisa came home from Hebrew Academy to tell me that they needed mothers to drive students to visit a kosher bakery. She asked if I could volunteer. I was glad to help. That day, while walking through the Fairfax area, I noticed that in the window of the Chabad bookstore there were some anti-missionary books on display. When no one was looking, I dashed back to the bookstore and bought every anti-missionary book available.

I was becoming more and more disturbed by my research. To this point I had studied in private. Only my family knew what I was reading. But the time had come for outside help, and so I turned to my rabbi. I called Mendel and Rochel and asked them to come to my home. When they arrived, we sat in the library, and I showed them my books. I told them that when I read my Bible, I saw Jesus. I asked Mendel to help me. They whispered to each other. Then they turned to me, and Mendel said, "Not to worry." He had just the man for me—a professional who works with people like myself. He would give him my phone number, and the man would call me. I thanked them as they left. I felt so grateful and relieved that I was going to get the help I needed and the answers I so desperately wanted.

> **I told them that when I
> read my Bible, I saw Jesus.**

Two nights later I received a phone call from Rabbi Ben Tzion Kravitz. I gave him a little background about my research and explained how it began. He listened and told me not to worry. He even mentioned a videotape he possessed of people who had renounced their faith in Jesus. I told him to bring it with him when he came to my house.

It was a lovely, sunny, clear morning when Rabbi Kravitz came to my house. I had prepared fresh fruit on a paper plate for the rabbi. I wanted him to know that I was familiar with the Laws of Kashrut, but would honor his hesitancy to eat anything away from his home. I did not wish to cause him any concern about what he was served.

When the rabbi arrived, I introduced him to Ron, who then retired to the upstairs where he spent the day working. Ron remained at home, not because I feared the rabbi, but because it was not appropriate for the rabbi and me to be alone.

For the next ten hours, the rabbi and I discussed the Bible, Jewish history, and tradition. The rabbi had a very modern approach to the Scriptures, and I, a very traditional one. After reading the Talmud, Midrash, Targumim, and other commentaries, I wanted to talk about what our forefathers believed and what the ancient Jewish writings had to say concerning the Messiah.

Desperately Seeking the Truth

After many conversations, the rabbi suggested I talk to someone else. He recommended Gerald Sigal in Brooklyn, New York, author of *The Jew and the Christian Missionary*. Rabbi Kravitz said he would call Mr. Sigal, tell him my situation, and let the two of us discuss various issues over the phone.

The rabbi and Mr. Sigal devised a plan. Mr. Sigal would call collect every Monday night. We would discuss various topics, and then he would pose a question that I would research during the week. The following Monday I would give him the answer.

For example, one week Mr. Sigal said that the genealogy of Jesus was faulty because, in Judaism, no women were ever included in the Jewish genealogies. I was puzzled by this statement for I had recently read the long list of genealogies in First Chronicles in Historical Records of the Jewish Bible, and women are mentioned in those records. The women's names were included to further the specific knowledge needed where a father had only daughters and no sons, or when there was more than one wife or there were concubines.

Our conversations continued for some time until Mr. Sigal told Rabbi Kravitz I was "too far gone" to be helped. Rabbi Kravitz was upset with me and said I should have accepted whatever Mr. Sigal said. He accused me of not really wanting to know the truth. The rabbi didn't understand I was desperately seeking the truth and would go to any lengths to find it. Rabbi Kravitz was probably embarrassed too because Rabbi Duchman kept asking him, "Haven't you helped her yet?"

When I Read My Bible I See "That Man"!

A short time after this, I received a phone call from Rabbi Duchman. He told me about an internationally known deprogrammer, Rabbi J. Immanuel Schochet, who would be speaking soon at my daughter's Yeshiva. I said I would attend.

The night I heard Rabbi Schochet proved to be a turning point in my search for the truth. My family and I sat up front because my daughter was attending the academy, and we felt comfortable sitting close to the speaker.

Earlier that evening Ron, Elisa, and I had decided that we would just go to listen, and we wouldn't say anything until the entire program was over. Then, and only then, would I quietly go up to the rabbi and ask him if he could help me.

The rabbi's speech centered on the generalities of Jewish home life and the problems facing the family. He also discussed various religions and how they differed from Judaism.

After the rabbi completed his talk, he asked for questions. One person asked the rabbi what he could do to protect his children from Christian influence. The rabbi stated that if traditions were respected and followed within a Jewish home, there would be less of a chance for a child to go astray.

Another person expressed his concern about missionaries who wanted to teach his children about Jesus. The rabbi reiterated the value of having Jewish traditions in the home, but also stressed the importance of sending our children to Jewish day schools and Yeshivas.

The third question came from a man who asked what he should do when his child comes home asking him about Scriptures with which he as a Jewish parent is not familiar.

At this point, Rabbi Schochet grabbed the sides of the podium and shouted to the audience, "Never under any circumstances does a knowledgeable Jew ever turn to That Man!" ("That Man" is a name that Jews call Jesus when they don't want to say His name.)

I felt the rabbi was talking directly to me, so I grabbed Ron's hand and whispered, "Should I say something?!"

And Ron said, "Yes!"

I then grabbed Elisa's hand and whispered, "Should I say something?!"

And Elisa said, "Yes!"

So I raised my hand and asked, "Rabbi, what do you tell someone like me who knows Yiddishkeit, follows Judaism, has a Jewish home, and yet, when I read the Jewish Bible, I see *That Man!!?*"

With so many Jewish families and rabbis in the room, my question hit like a bombshell. For the next four or five hours until midnight, Rabbi Schochet and I discussed Yiddishkeit, Jewish customs, the Bible, and other subjects. When midnight approached, the rabbi was anxious to close the meeting, so he said what he considered to be the words that would show me and all the others in the room why Jesus could not be the promised Messiah. He shouted to the audience that Jesus committed blasphemy from the cross.

Then in an angry, mocking tone, the rabbi quoted Jesus saying, "My God, My God, Why hast Thou forsaken Me?"

I was horrified at Rabbi Schochet's tone of voice and accusation that Jesus had committed blasphemy. I told him there were many ways that Jesus could have made that statement. He could have cried out in a plaintive voice or in a pleading or beseeching voice. But Rabbi Schochet refused to see my point of view. I found it amazing that in his anger, he apparently forgot that the statement Jesus made on the cross was first said by our own beloved King David in Psalm 22. *And would any Jew dare to say that David committed blasphemy?!*

> **That night I told my husband and daughter, "I have no more doubts... Jesus is my Jewish Messiah."**

I do not profess to be a Hebrew scholar or a Bible scholar. I am only a plain, ordinary Jewish woman who loves Yiddishkeit and who just wanted to know the truth.

That night I told my husband and daughter, "I have no more doubts...Jesus is my Jewish Messiah."

Commentary by Sid Roth

There are three major reasons some Jewish people don't investigate the claims of Jesus as Messiah. First, the most anti-Semitic people, historically, have called themselves Christians. By definition, the name "Christian" means a follower of the Messiah. Any person who is prejudiced and violent is the farthest thing from being a follower of the Messiah. These "Christians" may have worn large crosses and attended church, but their actions proved they were not followers of the Messiah, the Prince of Peace.

Second, we Jews believe in One God. Believers in the Messiah also believe in One God. But God's essence is infinite, beyond complete comprehension. The rabbis even called Him the *Eyn Sof*—the One Without End. From the Scriptures, we understand our One God can manifest Himself in more than one way. There is much evidence of this in the Torah. Did you ever wonder who was with God when He made man?—"Let *Us* make man in *Our* image, after *Our* likeness…" (Gen. 1:26).

My favorite passage that illustrates this unique nature is Genesis 19:24: "And the *Lord* rained upon Sodom and upon Gomorrah brimstone and fire, from the *Lord,* out of heaven." How could the Lord be in Heaven and also on earth simultaneously? Why must the One true God be as limited as man?

Incidentally, I don't pray to the Messiah; *I pray to God in the Name of the Messiah.* My forefathers prayed to God through the Jewish high priest. My High Priest is Jesus.

The last reason some Jewish people don't seek after Jesus is because the rabbis tell them if they believe in Jesus, they will no longer be Jewish. But if Jesus is the Jewish Messiah, then *there is nothing more Jewish than believing in Him.* So the question is not, How can you be Jewish and believe in Jesus? but rather, Who is Jesus?

The followers of Rabbi Schneerson that Sharon mentioned could have saved themselves a lot of trouble if they had thought for themselves. The Messiah had to be born in Bethlehem according to our Scriptures. Rabbi Schneerson never even *visited* Israel!

In fact, all rabbis worldwide could save themselves a lot of trouble if they understood why Rabbi Yochanon Ben Zakkai, the architect of modern-day rabbinic Judaism, didn't know whether he personally would go to Heaven or hell. A famous rabbi said, "If a blind man follows another blind man, won't both fall into a ditch?"

Is there life after death? With all the books about people who have died or had near-death experiences and gone to Heaven or hell, there can be little doubt. But what do our Jewish Scriptures tell us about life after death?

Daniel 12:1-2 says,

> *At that time shall thy people be delivered, every one that shall be found written in the book [of life]. And many of those that sleep in the dust of the earth shall awake, some to everlasting life, and some to disgrace and everlasting abhorrence.*

Only those whose names are recorded in the book of life go to everlasting life in Heaven. Is your name in the book of life? If you don't know for sure before you die, your fate is everlasting abhorrence (hell). The only way to know for sure is to know God. Not know about Him. Not just believe in Him. You must *know* Him. You must think for yourself.

Chapter 6
by Sid Roth

CHAPTER 6

There Must Be Something More!

"**B**ecause I work, eat, sleep, and that's the way it goes. There must be something more." These are the words of a song that I wrote shortly after graduating from college.

It seems as though I blinked my eyes, and I was married. I blinked my eyes again, and I had a daughter. I blinked my eyes again, and I had a job as a stockbroker with the largest brokerage firm in the world, Merrill Lynch. But there was something missing. Deep inside I felt a yearning—there had to be something more!

I didn't find it in religion. Both of my parents were Jewish. I attended an Orthodox synagogue and was bar mitzvahed. I was proud of being a Jew. But I found the religion boring and many of the religious people hypocritical. God was just not relevant in my life.

I was proud of being a Jew. But I found the religion boring and many of the religious people hypocritical.

So I looked to money for happiness. My goal was to become a millionaire by age 30. But I blinked my eyes again, and I was 29 with no hope of being a millionaire by 30.

I left my wife, my daughter, my job, and went searching for something more. I had been married young. Perhaps the single life would give me satisfaction. After one year, I knew this was not my answer. Then I took a New Age meditation course. The instructor taught me how to lower my brain waves. When I was in this passive, hypnotic state, I was told to invite a "counselor" into my head. He said this counselor would answer my questions.

On the last day of the course, the instructor tested my new power by giving me the name of a woman I didn't know. Then he asked what was physically wrong with her. I asked my counselor, and he showed me that this woman had cancer of the breast. "Could she have cancer of the breast?" I asked. My answer was correct. I knew it was not a lucky guess.

The power started growing. One day I had the thought, *I would like to open my own investment business.* Almost immediately, a businessman whom I barely knew offered me a free office, secretary, and telephone.

**"Sid, did you know your
own Jewish Bible condemns
your involvement in the occult?"**

Soon after I took advantage of his offer, he asked, "Sid, did you know your own Jewish Bible condemns your involvement in the occult?" He showed me from the Torah, Deuteronomy 18:10-12:

> *There shall not be found among thee any one who causeth his son or his daughter to pass through the fire [child sacrifice], one who useth divination [fortune telling], one who is an observer of times [astrology], or an enchanter [sorcery or omens], or a conjurer [hypnotist, witch]. Or a charmer [casts a magic spell], or a consulter with familiar spirits [medium or someone using channeling or ouija boards], or a wizard [spiritist, Transcendental Meditation, Silva Mind Control, Edgar Cayce], or who inquireth of the dead [channeling, seances, etc.]. For an abomination unto the Lord are all that do these things....*

This businessman told me that the "counselor" who gave me information was a demon and very evil.

The Bible, the Supernatural, and the Jews

Then I read a book by McCandlish Phillips called *The Bible, the Supernatural, and the Jews.*[1] Phillips said that because a Jew is under a covenant with God, he faces an even worse judgment for participating in New Age practices. The book included stories of famous Jewish people who had dabbled in the New Age—and lost their lives.

I decided I had better find out if the Bible really was from God. So I stopped consulting my counselor and started reading the Bible. I soon got the scare of my life. My counselor started cursing me. I realized this counselor had a mind of its own and was from the pit of hell. I *had* to get rid of it. But there was no one I could go to for help.

Then things got worse. I broke into astral projection. This is when your spirit leaves your body. I was afraid my spirit would be unable to find its way back and that my body would be buried alive.

As a young boy I had a great fear of death because I thought that dying meant I would cease to exist. Now death looked like my only way to find relief from this horrible situation.

The Worst Night of My Life

On the worst night of my life, I called my wife and asked her to pray. Then I prayed a prayer of my own: "Jesus, help!" I didn't know if He was real, but I had nowhere else to turn. When I went to bed, I didn't want to wake up. Life was too hard.

The next morning I knew immediately something was different. The evil that had been inside of me was gone. I knew it had to do with that prayer. Suddenly I realized I had no fear. Instead, I felt surrounded by liquid love. Finally I had experienced what the New Age could never give me—the tangible presence of God. I had never felt such peace. And I was convinced that Jesus was my Messiah.

Next I heard the audible voice of God. He told me to return to my wife and daughter. My wife, Joy, had become an agnostic when she was exposed to atheistic professors in college. But when I showed her the predictions about the Jewish people written thousands of years in advance in the Bible, she said, "I must believe the Bible is from God." (See Chapter 10 for further discussion about these predictions.) She became a believer in Jesus shortly thereafter.

Something Wrong With the Rabbi

My mother, a great peacemaker, convinced my father that my newfound belief in Jesus was a phase and it too would pass. I was very concerned for my parents to know the Messiah, and I tried to witness at every opportunity. My mother would listen, but my father would get angry and close his ears. Over the years my parents watched how my marriage was restored. They observed the new stability in my life. They could see I was becoming a real *mensch* (Yiddish word that, roughly translated, means "a good human"). They watched my wife, daughter, sister, brother-in-law, and nephews become believers. When my sister lost her daughter, Cheryl Ann, my parents observed her inner strength in dealing with this tragedy—a strength she had not had previously.

> **My mother, a great peacemaker, convinced my father that my newfound belief in Jesus was a phase and it too would pass.**

One day, after much prayer, my father let me read to him the 53rd chapter of Isaiah. By the time I finished, he was angry and accused me of reading from a Christian Bible because he said I was reading about Jesus. I showed him it was published by the Hebrew Publishing Company, but that was not good enough. He said he would only accept a Bible from his Orthodox rabbi. *Hmm,* I thought, *My father thinks Isaiah is speaking of Jesus.*

So the next day I called our family rabbi for an appointment. When I entered his office, he greeted me with a warm welcome and asked what he could do for me. I asked if he would give me a Bible and inscribe something personal to me. He gladly complied, writing some kind words to me on the inside cover.

I thanked him and left quickly. I could not wait to show this powerful gift to my father. When I arrived, I confidently displayed the inscription to my dad and made sure he read it. Then I began to read the same passage from Isaiah. Now he had only two choices. Either he had to agree Jesus was the Messiah, or he had to think something was wrong with the rabbi. To my shock, he said, "I've always thought there was something wrong with that rabbi." And then he proceeded to tell me how he once saw the rabbi eating out in a restaurant on Yom Kippur—the day of fasting.

Think for Yourself

One afternoon when I went over to my parents' house for a visit, my father was at the racetrack. I decided this was the time to prove to my mother that Jesus was the Messiah. I knew that she had very little knowledge of the Scriptures, did not know if they were true, and gave no thought to an afterlife, although she came from a religious family and attended an Orthodox synagogue.

> **"Mom, did you know the entire history of the Jewish people—past, present, and future—is in the Bible?...**

I started by trying to prove that there is a God and the Bible is His book: "Mom, did you know the entire history of the Jewish people—past, present, and future—is in the Bible? Hundreds of precise predictions have come true already. And the scientific dating of the Dead Sea Scrolls in Israel proves no one entered these predictions in the Bible after the event occurred.

"For instance, God said He would bless us beyond any people that ever lived, if we would be obedient to His laws (see Deut. 28:1). However, if we disobeyed, we would lose our country, be persecuted and scattered to the four corners of the earth (see Deut. 28:36-37; Isa. 11:12). And wherever we would flee, we would be persecuted (see Deut. 28:65). And, even though many of us would suffer and die, we would always be preserved as a distinct people (see Jer. 31:36). With the suffering we have gone through as Jews, you would think every Jew left alive would have assimilated as a means of self preservation. But against impossible odds, God has preserved us as a distinct people.

"Then, in the last days a miracle would happen. Israel would become a Jewish nation (see Jer. 16:15). If there were no Israel and the UN had to vote on it becoming a Jewish homeland today, what would the probability be? Zero would be too generous. That is how impossible it was in 1948. But God caused a great sign to occur that was of far greater magnitude than the crossing of the Red Sea as though it were dry land (see Jer. 16:14-15). And a nation, Israel, was formed in a day as Isaiah predicted (see Isa. 66:8).

"Amos said once we returned we would *rebuild* the waste cities (see Amos 9:14). And, if you investigate the history of Israel, you will find one city is built upon another. Tel Aviv is as modern and cosmopolitan as any city in the world. Isaiah even said the desert would blossom as the rose (see Isa. 35:1). By the way, did you know Israel exports more *roses* to Europe than any other nation? Ezekiel prophesied the reforestation of Israel (see Ezek. 36:8). And Isaiah 35:7 tells us, 'The burning sand will become a pool, the thirsty ground bubbling springs.' How did Isaiah know 2,700 years ago that Israel would develop technology that would cause underground water to bubble to the surface supporting the growth of vegetation in the barren desert? Since this water originates from deep within the earth, it comes out warm, allowing growth in any weather![2]

"The only way Isaiah or any of the other prophets could have known these things is if God told them. Two hundred years before Cyrus was born, Isaiah identifies him by name and says God would use this Gentile to build the Jewish Temple and restore the cities in Israel (see Isa. 44:28; 45:1,13). How did Isaiah know his name? And better still, how did God get a heathen to want to restore Jerusalem? Jeremiah prophesied that Israel would go into captivity in Babylon for exactly 70 years (see Jer. 29:10). Guess how many years we were captive in Babylon?

"I could go on and on about the amazing predictions of the Bible that were written thousands of years before the fact, but would you like to know about our future? Since God has demonstrated 100 percent accuracy so far, it is reasonable to expect Him to know our future."

> **...for the first time in her life, she was confronted with the accuracy of God's Word.**

As I quickly moved from Scripture to Scripture, I could tell my mother was impressed with my knowledge of the

Bible. And for the first time in her life, she was confronted with the accuracy of God's Word.

"Mom, Zechariah says that in the last days the whole world will not know what to do with Jerusalem (see Zech. 12:3). Today, the problems of Jerusalem and the tiny nation of Israel are in the news continuously. And Israel will be invaded by many nations. The invading powers are mentioned by name (see Ezek. 38:3-9). It will be a real blood bath; two-thirds of our people will perish (see Zech. 13:8). And when there is no hope left, the Messiah will fight for Israel. Let me read it to you from Zechariah:

> Then the Lord will go out and fight against those nations, as He fights in the day of battle ... "They [the Jewish people] will look on Me, the one they have pierced, and they will mourn for Him as one mourns for an only child, and grieve bitterly for Him as one grieves for a firstborn son. On that day the weeping in Jerusalem will be great ..."
> (Zechariah 14:3; 12:10-11).

"Mom, do you know why we will be weeping?" I think this was the first time I paused for air and gave her a chance to speak.

"I guess because we will be so grateful for being spared," she said.

"That is partially right. But the main reason is that we will realize, for the first time, that Jesus is our Messiah, and we missed Him."

"But if Jesus is the Messiah, why don't all the rabbis believe? Sidney, I love you, but you still don't know as much as the rabbis who have studied all their life."

"Mom, the Talmud tells us that years ago, when the rabbis pondered how to recognize the Messiah, they concluded that there would be *two* Messiahs. One would suffer for the people and be like Joseph. He would be rejected by his own people. He is described in Isaiah 53:

> *He was despised and rejected by men, a man of sorrows, and familiar with suffering. Like one from whom men hide their faces He was despised, and we esteemed Him not* (Isaiah 53:3).

"And, according to Daniel 9:26, He would die before the second Temple was destroyed:

> *After the sixty-two 'sevens,' the Anointed One [the Messiah] will be cut off and will have nothing. The people of the ruler who will come will destroy the city and the sanctuary.*

"He would die by crucifixion. David describes this hundreds of years before the first recorded crucifixion. David even saw the guards gambling for his clothes. And he noted that His bones would not be broken because this is the requirement for acceptable sacrifices.

> *I am poured out like water, and all My bones are out of joint. My heart has turned to wax; it has melted away within Me. My strength is dried up like a potsherd, and My tongue sticks to the roof of My mouth; you lay Me in the dust of death.... They have pierced My hands and My feet. I can count all My bones; people stare and gloat over me. They divide My garments among them and cast lots for My clothing* (Psalm 22:14-18).

"He did not die for His own sins but for *our sins*:

> *...we considered Him stricken by God, smitten by Him, and afflicted. But He was pierced for our transgressions, He was crushed for our iniquities; the punishment that brought us peace was upon Him, and by His wounds we are healed* (Isaiah 53:4-5).

"Incidentally, the prophets go on to say His ancestry would be from the line of David (see 2 Sam. 7:12-13); the Gentiles would follow Him (see Isa. 11:10); and He would be born in Bethlehem of Judah (see Micah 5:2). Did you know his mother was living in the wrong place until shortly before His birth? Mary had to go to Bethlehem for a special census for tax purposes at the precise moment of his birth!"

"OK already, so why don't the rabbis see this?" she asked.

"Well, they saw this suffering servant Messiah and called Him 'Messiah ben (son of) Joseph.' But then they found just as many predictions about the Messiah reigning as King and ushering in an age of peace. They called Him 'Messiah ben David,' like King David. How did they reconcile these supposedly contradictory roles? Their theory was that there were two distinct Messiahs. But today it is clear that it is *one* Messiah with *two* appearances. First, he came to initiate the New Covenant prophesied by Jeremiah, to change us from the inside out.

"OK already, so why don't the rabbis see this?" she asked.

*"The time is coming," declares the Lord, "when
I will make a new covenant with the house of
Israel ... and will remember their sins no more"*
(Jeremiah 31:31,34).

"Since we humans are so unclean compared to the holiness of God, we always needed a mediator and the blood of an innocent animal to atone for our sins. During Temple days our intermediary was a high priest. Today our intermediary cleanses us from all sins, the Lamb of God who takes away the sins of the whole world. Then, when we are clean, He actually takes up residence inside our body, which becomes His temple.

"Speaking of two appearances of the Messiah, did you know the first time Moses identified himself as our deliverer we rejected him? (See Exodus 2:11-14.) And the first time Joseph identified himself as our deliverer, his own brothers wanted to kill him (see Gen. 37:8,19-20). Jesus fits this same pattern. His second appearance will be when He comes to rule the world and to usher in an age of peace.

*They will neither harm nor destroy on all My
holy mountain, for the earth will be full of the
knowledge of the Lord as the waters cover the sea*
(Isaiah 11:9).

"Today the rabbis teach us about His second coming, but never mention Messiah Ben Joseph. I found out why when I participated in a debate with a rabbi at the University of Maryland. After the debate, I engaged a young Orthodox rabbinical student in dialogue. I asked him to tell me who Isaiah was speaking of in the 53rd chapter. He amazed me with his answer. He said, 'I can't tell you.'

"'Why?' I quickly asked. 'You know Hebrew better than I. Read it from your *Tanakh* (Old Covenant).'"

"'No,' he responded, 'it would be a sin.'"

"'Why?' I asked again."

"'Because I am not holy enough,' he said. 'We can only tell you what the rabbis who lived closer to the days of Moses tell us the verse means.'"

"How sad, Mom. What he was really saying was *he could not think for himself.*"

Although I thought my presentation to my mother was overwhelming, she let me know she was grateful for the change believing in Jesus had caused in my life, but was not ready to accept the truth. "What would your father say? Are you hungry? Can I get you something to eat?"

> **Over the years, whenever my mother was sick, I would pray for her, and God would heal her. …Before she died, she too accepted *Yeshua* (Hebrew for Jesus) as her Messiah.**

Over the years, whenever my mother was sick, I would pray for her, and God would heal her. As a Jewish nonbeliever, my mom was so proud of me she would tell all her Jewish friends that if they were sick her son would pray in

Jesus' Name, and God would heal them. Before she died, she too accepted *Yeshua* (Hebrew for Jesus) as her Messiah.

Who Is a True Jew?

But my dad was still embarrassed and very hurt by my faith. He was born in Poland and saw anti-Semitism by so-called "Christians" firsthand. After my mother's funeral, my father had only one question: Was I going to say the prayers (*Kaddish*) for my mother in the synagogue every day for eleven months? There was an ulterior motive behind my father's question. If I would say the prayers for my mother, he could be assured that I would say them for him. And it was his belief that somehow these prayers would be his ticket into Heaven without punishment or delay. Since he knew I did not agree with this form of prayer, he wondered what my answer would be. For a split second I thought of the time commitment. I thought of the endurance needed to sit through all the rituals and prayers in a language I did not understand. I thought of the possible repercussions by those in the synagogue who knew of my outspoken faith in Jesus. But as quickly as these thoughts raced through my mind, I found myself agreeing to do it.

It had been years since I had put on the *tefillin* (little box with Scripture inside that is wrapped around one's head and arm to conform to Deuteronomy 6:8). A retired rabbi helped me as I placed the tefillin around my arm and on my head.

After one service, I got into a conversation with the man who read from the Torah. The Torah reading happened to be about the Jewish people walking through the Red Sea as though it were dry land. As I discussed this with my friend, he looked at me with the most incredulous expression and said, "You don't really believe those stories, do you?"

I responded with just as incredulous an expression and said, "You don't? What are you doing here?"

It is one thing when a secular Jew does not believe in the Torah. But when a Jewish religious leader does not believe, it shocks me. Then, when he told me he did not believe in God or life after death, I was curious why he came to the synagogue at all. He responded, "Because my friends are here. Because I like the traditions of my fathers. And because it gives me something to do."

I always thought these elderly men who *davined* (prayed) every day at the *minyan* (a gathering of ten or more Jewish men to pray) were the most holy Jews in the synagogue. I found that many of the men I prayed with felt the same way as this man.

My father greatly appreciated my going to the synagogue every day to pray. And since I had not mentioned Jesus in a while, he asked, "Do you still believe in Him?" I had been waiting for God's timing because every time I mentioned Jesus, my father would always get angry. I told him that I believed in Jesus and He was the reason I was going to the synagogue. I said I did not believe the prayers were necessary for Mom because she was already in Heaven. At that, he got angry, and I quickly changed the subject.

> **My father would say to me,
> "You're a wonderful son.
> You're as good as gold. But do
> you have to believe in *Him?*"**

On another occasion my father said men from the synagogue had told him that their sons would not have been so faithful to go to the synagogue every day. My father would say to me, "You're a wonderful son. You're as good as gold. But do you have to believe in *Him?*"

The Talmud declares that if a voice from heaven should contradict the majority of rabbis, we must ignore that voice. A *true* Jew says that if the Torah contradicts the majority of the rabbis, we must follow the Torah.

May God grant that soon all Israel would be *true* Jews.

Heaven Must Be a Wonderful Place

Years later, I got a call that my father was dying in the hospital. My sister, also a believer, and I went to his bedside. I felt a strong presence of God that had been on me constantly for several days. It was the same tangible presence as when Jesus first became real to me years earlier. I said, "Dad, do you remember how Mom always said, 'Heaven must be a wonderful place'? Don't you want to be with her and the rest of our family?"

My father had lost his voice. His body was destroyed by cancer. But a great miracle happened. When I asked him if he wanted to make Yeshua his Messiah and Lord, my sister and I heard him say,

"Yes!"

I am a very thankful person. Every member of my immediate Jewish family believes in Yeshua. Joy and I have celebrated 52 years of marriage. My daughter is now married and has three daughters.

> **And I have seen miracles**
> **happen thousands of times when**
> **I pray for the sick in His name.**

It has been more than 40 years since I was set free. Over time, the mind can play tricks. If this had been my only experience with God, I would begin to doubt. But I have studied the Bible for myself, and I am 100 percent convinced only one person in all of history could be the Jewish Messiah. Daily I experience the presence of God. And I have seen miracles happen thousands of times when I pray for the sick in His name.

Thank God there is something more!

Now It's Your Turn

Many believe they are basically "good" because they have a "good" heart. God says differently: "The heart is deceitful above all things, and desperately wicked..."

(Jeremiah 17:9). But God loved us too much to leave us in that condition.

This is why He says through His Jewish prophet Ezekiel: "I will sprinkle clean water on you, and you will be clean. Your filth will be washed away.... And I will give you a new heart, and I will put a new spirit in you. I will take out your stony, stubborn heart and give you a tender, responsive heart" (Ezekiel 36:25-26 NLT).

The Messiah came to earth the first time to suffer and pay the penalty for our sins. He will come a second time to usher in an age of peace on earth. How could we ever have peace on earth with wicked hearts? We all need a heart transplant.

God wants to give *you* a new heart filled with His love and to place His Spirit inside you. Some, like me, will have a dramatic encounter when they receive a new heart. Others will accept this forgiveness by faith. My wife felt nothing when she first prayed to God for a new heart, but as time went by, she realized she had changed and God was living inside of her.

It is also important to read the Bible. I would start with the New Testament. This will cause you to grow rapidly in the knowledge of the Messiah.

Now say this prayer out loud and believe it to the best of your ability:

"Dear God, I confess that I have sinned against You, and I am truly sorry for it. Messiah Yeshua, please come into my heart and life and cleanse me with

Your precious blood of atonement. Give me a new heart filled with Your love. In Yeshua's Name, Amen."

Endnotes

1. McCandlish Philips, *The Bible, the Supernatural, and the Jews* (New York, NY: World Pub. Co., 1970).

2. From an interview with Dr. Dov Pasternack of the Ben Gurion University of the Negev on "Report to Zion," *Messianic Vision* radio broadcast #8 (April 1989).

CHAPTER 7
BY MICHAEL L. BROWN, PH.D.

CHAPTER 7

Tradition or Truth? What I Learned About Rabbinic Judaism

"**Y**ou don't even know Hebrew! How can you tell me what the Bible says?"

"It's true, Rabbi. I don't know Hebrew—but I *will* learn. In the meantime, I can use the dictionary in the back of Strong's Concordance."

"Meantime, shmeantime. If you don't know Hebrew, it doesn't mean a thing."

I will never forget those words spoken to me in 1972. I was a brand-new believer in Jesus, just 17 years old. My life had been *dramatically* changed—and I mean dramatically. Only months before, I was shooting heroin, using massive quantities of LSD and speed, and living in total, reckless abandon. My nickname, "Drug Bear," was well deserved, and I was sinful, proud, and rotten to the core. All this was in spite of a typical, Long Island, Conservative Jewish upbringing by very happily married parents. In fact, my father was a highly respected lawyer working as the Senior Law Assistant to the New York State Supreme Court judges.

My drug abuse was not due to some inner turmoil or spiritual quest. I used drugs because they made me feel good! You see, I was a fairly talented, teenage rock drummer, and the whole Woodstock, cast-off-restraint, get high, do-your-own-thing mentality appealed to me. I wanted to be like the rock stars! Soon, life became one big party.

The Surprise of My Life

But God had other plans. My two best friends (the bass player and guitar player in our band) were raised in homes that were "Christian" in name only. They were no closer to Jesus than I was. But they were friendly with two girls whose father was a dedicated, "born-again" Christian, and their uncle pastored a little church in Queens, New York. The girls went to the church to please their father, my friends went to the church to spend time with the girls, and then I went to the church to pull them all out. I didn't like the changes I was beginning to see in them!

What happened? I got the surprise of my life. In that little church, I met with the God I was not seeking, and I found out the truth about Jesus, the Savior and Messiah in whom I had never believed. I was transformed! The love of God broke down my resistance, and in answer to the secret prayers of a faithful few, I turned away from the filthy life I had been leading. My father was thrilled to see the change.

He had only one problem: "We're Jewish! Now that you are free from drugs, you need to meet the rabbi and come back to our traditions." And so, I began to talk with the young, scholarly rabbi who had just become the spiritual leader of the synagogue in which I was bar mitzvahed.

I Must Learn Hebrew

I knew beyond any doubt that my experience was real, but how could I answer his questions? What could I say when he told me that the English translation I was using was wrong, and that, time and time again, the New Testament writers misinterpreted the Hebrew Scriptures? He could read the original text. I couldn't! He also brought me to meet with Ultra-Orthodox, Lubavitcher rabbis in Brooklyn who specialized in dealing with "straying" young Jews like me. For my part, I was happy to have the opportunity to share my faith with these sincere men. After all, I was reading the Bible day and night, memorizing hundreds of verses, praying for hours, even persuading a Jewish Jehovah's Witness that her religion was not biblical. But these rabbis in Brooklyn had answers I had never heard before. And all of them had been able to read and understand Hebrew since their childhood. I could barely remember how to pronounce the letters! Plus, they *looked* so Jewish, with long black beards and all. Their faith seemed to be so ancient and authentic. Was mine?

So it was that I began to study Hebrew in college. If my faith was based on truth, it could withstand honest academic scrutiny. If Jesus was really the Jewish Messiah, I had nothing to fear. Serious questions deserved serious answers, and I was determined to follow the truth wherever it led, regardless of the consequences.

> **If Jesus was really the Jewish Messiah, I had nothing to fear. Serious questions deserved serious answers...**

Little by little, I became convinced that I should pursue scholarly biblical and Jewish studies. One year in college I took only language courses, *six* to be exact: Hebrew, Arabic, Greek, Latin, German, and Yiddish. Talk about brain drain! I wanted to read the relevant texts for myself, in the original languages, without anyone's help.

But college was not enough. In order to pursue my goals, graduate school was necessary. There I could study the other ancient languages relevant to the Hebrew Scriptures, languages like Akkadian (that is, Babylonian and Assyrian), Ugaritic (from a major city north of Canaan), Aramaic, Syriac, Phoenician, Punic, Moabite— the list goes on. By the time I wrote my doctoral dissertation, I had studied about 15 languages, some in great depth, others only superficially. I received my Ph.D. from New York University in Near Eastern languages.

Faulty Foundations

Almost all my courses were taught by Jewish professors and, along the way, I also had the opportunity to do some private study with several rabbis. What happened to my faith? It actually became *stronger*. As I learned more, I became even more convinced that Jesus was the prophesied Messiah, the one whose life, atoning death, resurrection, and return were foreshadowed in the Hebrew Scriptures. I had sound answers for serious questions!

I also discovered something unexpected: It was not the New Testament faith that was built on faulty foundations; the foundations of *rabbinic Judaism* were faulty! It was rabbinic Judaism, not the New Testament faith, that deviated from the Hebrew Bible.

> **It was not the New Testament
> faith that was built on faulty
> foundations; the foundations
> of *rabbinic Judaism* were faulty!**

Rabbinic Judaism does not even claim to be based upon a literal interpretation of the Scriptures. Instead, the rabbis say that their faith is the continuation of an unbroken chain of *tradition* dating back to Moses and the prophets. This is a crucial point. As we will see later, such an unbroken chain does not exist.

I have often heard rabbis and anti-missionaries say—in a somewhat derogatory tone—that without Christ there could be no Christianity (or, without Messiah there could be no Messianic Judaism), whereas Judaism can exist without a Messiah, important as such a figure is in Jewish thinking. Judaism, it is claimed, is the religion of the Torah.

Of course, I agree that there could be no Christianity without a Christ, just as I agree that there could be no salvation without a Savior and no deliverance without a Deliverer. This presents no problem at all. Our faith is based on the person and work of the Messiah.

But the real question is the following: on what foundation is traditional Judaism based? Judaism as we know it today is not the religion of the Torah as much as it is *the religion of rabbinic tradition*. Without tradition, there could be no traditional Judaism; without the rabbis, there could be no rabbinic Judaism. This is very significant! For many of our people, human tradition is more important than biblical truth.

More than 20 years ago, an Orthodox rabbi told me I was reading the Scriptures through rose-colored glasses. In other words, I would always misunderstand the Word no matter how sincere I tried to be. I wasn't seeing clearly. My vision was distorted.

> **More than 20 years ago, an Orthodox rabbi told me I was reading the Scriptures through rose-colored glasses.**

That was quite an accusation, and I didn't take it lightly. I studied the Word from every possible angle, asking myself whether other interpretations were correct, challenging the standard Christian answers with which I was familiar. Now, almost a quarter of a century later, I can honestly say that it is religious Jews—in spite of their sincerity and devotion—who read the Bible with colored glasses. They will be the first to tell you that *the Bible says only what the sages tell them it says.*

Who are they to differ with the great Jewish teachers of the past? Who are they to disagree with the famous rabbinic commentaries of the middle ages? How could they possibly break with the traditions they learned from their fathers? "After all, what can I know? My father learned it from his father who learned it from his father, who learned it from his father, and so on, all the way back to Moses. Are you telling me they made it up? Are you telling me they were deceived? How dare you question our sacred traditions!"

And so the myth of an unbroken chain of tradition going back to Moses has kept many Jewish people from reading the Bible on their own. This is the heart of the matter.

The Game of Telephone

Rabbinic Judaism believes that God gave Moses a Written Law (found in the Torah, the five books of Moses). But, we are told, most of the commandments in the Law are briefly worded, general statements, something like the headings of a paragraph in a book. They need interpretation. They need to be expanded and explained. So, according to the traditional belief, God also gave Moses an Oral

Law that interpreted the Written Law. Moses then passed this on to Joshua, who passed it on to the 70 leading elders in his generation, who passed it on to the prophets of the next generations.

And so it went, but not without lots of additions. This is because the rabbis teach that the Oral Law kept growing, since in every generation, new traditions were developed and new situations emerged which called for new applications of the Law.

Within two centuries after the time of Jesus, this Oral Law was so bulky and complex that it had to be written down lest it be forgotten (that's right, the basics of the *Oral* Law were now *written*). This became the Mishnah, which was expanded into what is known as the Talmud over the next few centuries. After that, according to the rabbinic belief, those who studied the Talmud continued to develop and pass down the Oral Law to each succeeding generation. *Every religious Jew believes with all his heart that it is impossible to understand the Scriptures or follow God's Law without these oral traditions.*

And what happens when an observant Jew is approached by a Jewish believer in Jesus? The believer is regarded as an ignorant newcomer, and his interpretations are totally scorned: "We have an unbroken tradition going back to Moses! How dare you differ with us! How dare you try to teach us!" Yes, tradition carries quite a lot of weight. And it can stop people from thinking for themselves. (I find it amusing, to say the least, when Orthodox Jews tell me that *I* have been brainwashed!)

> **What happens when an observant Jew is approached by a Jewish believer in Jesus? The believer is regarded as an ignorant newcomer, and his interpretations are totally scorned...**

Now you can better understand why so many Jews with whom believers try to dialog will immediately say: "I have to ask my rabbi. He will tell me what that verse really means. He will look it up in his books." You see, the rabbinic Jew believes that the further back in time you go, the closer you get to the original revelation at Mount Sinai (kind of like a thirty-five-hundred-year-old game of "telephone"). And Talmudic tradition teaches that, since the days of Moses, we have been on a steady spiritual decline. This is all the more reason that we have to depend on the views of the earlier generations! They were closer to those who received the original revelation, and they were on a higher spiritual plane. *They* can tell us what the Scripture means. Talk about reading the Bible through colored glasses!

Are the Traditions True?

"But," someone might ask, "how can you be so sure that these traditions aren't true? Why do you say that they don't provide the correct interpretations?" The answers are simple: 1) They take for themselves an authority that the Scriptures never gave them. 2) They put the voice of earthly reason on a higher plane than the prophetic word from Heaven. 3) They contradict the plain meaning of the Scriptures. 4) At times they even contradict the voice of God. 5) There is *no* biblical evidence for an unbroken chain of tradition and *plenty* of evidence against it.

Before I give you some examples, I want you to understand that this is not a matter of finding minor contradictions and interpretative difficulties. No. The issues here deal with the very heart and soul of traditional Judaism, a religion which stands or falls on its traditions.

The question that every honest Jew must ask is:

What if the Bible says one thing and my traditions say another? Will I follow God, or will I follow man?

It is not a question of whether these Jewish leaders were evil men and deceivers. Most of them were zealous for their faith. They sought to lead good lives and please the Lord. But were they right? Did their traditions really originate with God, or did they originate with man? Let's take a careful look. None of the examples that follow are taken out of context in any way. They are plain and straightforward.

First, let's see what traditional Judaism says of itself. According to the contemporary Orthodox scholar H. Chaim Schimmel, the Jewish people "*do not follow the literal word of the Bible,* nor have they ever done so. They have been fashioned and ruled by the verbal interpretation of the written word...."[1]

As expressed by Rabbi Z.H. Chajes, a leading 19th-century authority, the Talmud indicates that the words "that were transmitted orally" by God are "more valuable" than those transmitted in writing. Chajes goes so far as to say that

> allegiance to the authority of the said rab-
> binic tradition is binding upon all sons of
> Israel.... And he who does not give adher-
> ence to the unwritten Law and the rabbinic
> tradition has no right to share the heritage of
> Israel....[2]

How can such a claim be made? The rabbis assert that *it is the Bible itself* that gives them the exclusive authority to interpret Torah and develop new laws. They find support for this in Deuteronomy 17:8-12, probably the most impor-tant text in the Bible for rabbinic Judaism. This is what the verses say:

> *If cases come before your courts that are too diffi-
> cult for you to judge—whether bloodshed, law-
> suits, or assaults—take them to the place the Lord
> your God will choose. Go to the priests, who are
> Levites, and to the judge who is in office at that
> time. Inquire of them and they will give you the
> verdict. You must act according to the decisions
> they give you at the place the Lord will choose. Be
> careful to do everything they direct you to do. Act
> according to the law they teach you and the deci-
> sions they give you. Do not turn aside from what
> they tell you, to the right or to the left. The man
> who shows contempt for the judge or for the priest
> who stands ministering there to the Lord your*

God must be put to death. You must purge the evil
from Israel.

What Moses is clearly saying is that in every generation the Levitical priests and the current "judge" in Jerusalem would function as a kind of Supreme Court, a court of final appeal, the likes of which exist today in many nations around the world, including Israel and the United States. This court would be responsible for settling disputes regarding various legal matters such as homicide, civil law, and assaults. That's it! The text does not give any authority to subsequent generations of rabbis around the world (where does it even mention rabbis?), nor does it give *any-one* authority to tell all Jews when to pray, what to pray, how to slaughter their cattle, what to believe about the Messiah, when to visit the sick, whether or not one can write on the Sabbath, and on and on and on. Nothing of the sort! Yet, it is from this little text that the sages have derived so much power.

As for verse 11, which says, "Act according to the law they teach you and the decisions they give you. *Do not turn aside from what they tell you, to the right or to the left,*" this was actually interpreted by the 13th-century commentator Nachmanides to mean the following: "Even if it seems to you as if they are changing 'right' into 'left'...it is incumbent on you to think what they say is 'right' is 'right.'"[3] Why? Because the Spirit of God is on them, and the Lord will keep them from error and from stumbling. This is quite a claim! If the sages tell you that left is right, you are to follow the sages. Let's take this a step further. What if

1,000 prophets of the caliber of Elijah and Elisha tell you that the Torah means one thing, but 1,001 sages tell you it means something else? Whom do you follow? Maimonides, the most influential medieval Jewish scholar, is emphatic: "The final ruling is in accordance with the 1,001 sages."[4] Yes, the Talmud even teaches that if Elijah himself differed with a rabbinic *tradition* or a prevailing *custom* of the people—not a biblical Law itself but simply a tradition or custom concerning that Law—then he should not be followed.[5]

"But," you might say, "there may be something to that. Shouldn't we follow the plain and obvious meaning of the Bible even if some prophet claims that God told him otherwise?" Of course we should. But that is *not* what Maimonides was saying. He actually argued that if someone like Elijah favored the plain and obvious meaning of the Scriptures instead of the rabbinic tradition, the tradition was to be followed.

So even a proven prophet, backed by the power of God and following the plain sense of the Bible, has less weight than rabbinic tradition. And the sages, by a majority of even one, outweigh the likes of Elijah and Elisha when it comes to interpreting the Law. Are things getting clearer now?

More Weight—Rabbis or God?

But it doesn't stop there: A legal decision made by the majority of the sages *carries more weight than even the voice of God!* According to one of the most famous stories in the Talmud (Baba Mesia 59b), there was a dispute between

Rabbi Eliezer the Great and the sages about whether or not a particular kind of oven was ritually clean. He answered every one of their arguments, but they refused to accept his decision. Rabbi Eliezer then called upon a series of miracles to verify his ruling: If the Law is in accordance with me, then let this carob tree be uprooted; let this stream of water stop flowing; let the walls of this house of study collapse. Amazingly, the Talmud teaches that each miracle happened, but still the other rabbis refused to be moved.

Finally, Rabbi Eliezer called on God Himself to verify his position. Immediately, a voice came from Heaven saying, "Why are you troubling Rabbi Eliezer? The legal ruling is always in accordance with him." To which Rabbi Joshua exclaimed, "It is not in Heaven!" In other words, since the Torah was given at Mount Sinai (and is therefore no longer "in Heaven"), legal decisions are to be made solely on the basis of human reasoning and logical deduction. Period. As expressed by the legal authority Rabbi Aryeh Leib, "Let the truth emerge from the earth. The truth be as the sages decide with the human mind."[6]

And so if God speaks—as He did here—the sages can (and should!) overrule Him if they disagree with His interpretation. What was the basis for such an incredible position? The Talmud cites the last three words of Exodus 23:2 and interprets them to mean, "Follow the majority." But the text says the exact opposite! Just read the whole verse. The meaning is clearly, "*Don't* follow the majority." Even J. H. Hertz, the former chief rabbi of England, wrote, "The Rabbis disregarded the literal meaning of the last three

Hebrew words, and took them to imply that, except when it is 'to do evil,' one should follow the majority."[7]

And that is their support for negating and disregarding the voice of God! A verse that says "Don't follow the majority" was sliced up and reinterpreted so as to mean, "Follow the majority," and, on this basis, God Himself was overruled. It almost takes your breath away.

Can Rabbis Change the Torah?

Amazingly, the Talmudic text goes on to say that Elijah later informed one of the rabbis that God laughed about the incident saying, "My sons have defeated Me!" Talk about "majority rules"! Not only is it true that 1,000 prophets following the plain sense of the Scripture don't stand a chance against 1,001 sages, but God Himself doesn't stand a chance against even two sages should they beg to differ with Him! Did you have any idea that the power of tradition and human authority went so far?

> **Not only is it true that 1,000 prophets following the plain sense of the Scripture don't stand a chance against 1,001 sages, but God Himself doesn't stand a chance against even two sages should they beg to differ with Him!**

It is not that these rabbis were arrogant or irreverent. They simply believed that it was their God-given duty to interpret and make Laws, and, over the process of time, they came to believe that their traditions were sacred. They even claimed to have the right to *change* the biblical Laws if necessary. What was their scriptural support for this? Psalm 119:126: "It is time for you to act, O Lord; Your law is being broken." To which you might say, "I don't get it. What has this verse got to do with changing the Law?" Nothing. But it was totally reinterpreted (actually, totally *mis*interpreted) to mean: "Sometimes, in order to act for the Lord, it is necessary to dissolve His Laws."[8] I kid you not. Is it any wonder, then, that at times the Talmud credits the sages with "uprooting Scripture" with their interpretations?[9] This is something worth remembering the next time someone tries to tell you that Jesus and Paul freely went around breaking and changing the laws.

And where do the rabbis claim that the Bible itself makes reference to the Oral Law? One key text is Exodus 34:27:

> *Then the Lord said to Moses, "Write down these words, for in accordance with these words I have made a covenant with you and with Israel."*

What does this verse have to do with the *Oral* Law? Nothing at all! The context speaks of Laws to be *written down*.

How then did the authors of the Talmud find a reference here to the *unwritten* Law? First, they failed to quote the beginning of the verse ("*Write down* these words"). Then, they noticed that the Hebrew phrase translated "in accordance with" (*'al pî*) was very close to the Hebrew phrase for "oral" (*'al peh*). So, the verse was understood as if it said, "Write down these words, for on the testimony over these words, I have made a covenant with you and with Israel." But that is *not* what the Hebrew says, as any reliable Jewish translation of the Bible will tell you at once. A play on words is one thing; the real meaning is something else.

And how did Rashi, the greatest of all Jewish biblical commentators, handle the clear meaning of this verse that the covenant was based on the *written Word?* He interpreted "Write down these words" to mean *these words only*, explaining that "it is not permitted to write down the words of the Oral Law."[10] So, God says, "Write!" but the tradition says, "Don't write it all!" God makes His covenant with Israel based on what was transmitted in writing; the Talmud says that the real essence of the covenant was based on what was transmitted orally. And isn't it strange that a biblical text clearly emphasizing the *Written Law* was utilized by the Talmud to point to the *Oral Law*—based on a play on words alone? What an example of grasping at straws!

The complete absence of any mention of an Oral Law in the Hebrew Bible stands in direct contrast to the frequent references to the binding nature of the Written Law found throughout the Scriptures. Just read verses like Deuteronomy 31:24-26:

> *After Moses finished writing in a book the words of this law from beginning to end [and notice: there was no part of the Law that Moses failed to write down; he wrote it all, from beginning to end], he gave this command to the Levites who*

*carried the ark of the covenant of the Lord: "Take
this Book of the Law and place it beside the ark of
the covenant of the Lord your God. There it will
remain as a witness against you."*

There are plenty of other verses that say the same thing,
such as Exodus 24:7-8; Deuteronomy 17:14-20; 28:58-59;
30:9-10; Joshua 1:8; 23:6; First Kings 2:1-3; Second Kings
22:13; 23:3,21; First Chronicles 16:39-40; Second
Chronicles 30:5; 31:3; 35:26-27; Ezra 3:2-4; 6:18; Nehemiah
10:28-29; 13:1; and Daniel 9:13. I encourage you to look up
these verses and read them carefully. Where is there any
mention of an Oral Law?[11]

And if there were such an authoritative chain of interpretation, why are there so many disagreements about the
Law on virtually every page of the Talmud? One could
almost say that the Talmud *consists* of disagreements and
discussions about the interpretation and application of the
Law. And why do the great rabbinic commentaries differ on
the meaning of hundreds and hundreds of biblical verses?
Where is the authoritative chain of tradition?

> **And if there were such an authoritative
> chain of interpretation, why are there
> so many disagreements about the Law
> on virtually every page of the Talmud?**

No, God did not give an Oral Law to Moses on Mount
Sinai. The very first mention of even the *concept* of such a

binding, oral tradition is more than 1,400 years *after* Moses. What's more, many of the Jewish groups that existed in Jesus' day, such as the Sadducees and the Essenes, had no belief in any such tradition. That was a distinct doctrine of the Pharisees. Why? Because they were the ones who invented the whole idea of an unbroken chain of binding, oral tradition, beginning shortly before Jesus came into the world. And, as they passed their unique traditions on to their successors, the new generations began to say: "We didn't invent these teachings, we inherited them. They have been passed on to us from our fathers. They go back many years...way back...as far back as we can remember...all the way back to Moses." Not quite!

Let the truth be told. There was no secret Law given to Moses by word of mouth or passed on by him orally to the biblical prophets and leaders. Actually, our forefathers sometimes forgot the *Written Law* (read Second Kings 22 for a classic example of this). An *Oral Law* wouldn't have stood a chance. And there is not a single example in the Scriptures where anyone was ever punished, rebuked, or held accountable for breaking any so-called binding *tradition*. That's because there was no such tradition to break. Only violations of the written Word were considered sinful.

The Truth

Now it's time to listen to that Word. The Torah tells us that wherever we Jews are, even scattered around the world, "if from there you seek the Lord your God, you will find Him if you look for Him with all your heart and with all your soul" (Deut. 4:29). Jeremiah the prophet gave the same message: "You will seek Me and find Me when you seek Me with all your heart" (Jer. 29:13). And the Book of Proverbs says,

> *Trust in the Lord with all your heart and lean not on your own understanding; in all your ways acknowledge Him, and He will make your paths straight* (Proverbs 3:5-6).

God will not let you down—if you sincerely seek His truth. Why not humble yourself and ask for His help? There is a place for reason and rational discussion, and there is a place for seeking God too. They go hand in hand! But the Lord opposes those who are wise in their own eyes. Study the Word *and* seek God. You will not be disappointed.

When Moses and the prophets couldn't figure out how to interpret or apply the Law, they prayed and asked God for the answer. And God showed them what to do![12] Why not follow their lead? Why be smarter than Moses and the prophets and try to figure it all out for yourself?

> **Ask God to guide
> you into the truth.**

Study, yes, by all means. But ask God to open your eyes when you do! (That's exactly how the Psalmist prayed in Psalm 119:18.) Ask God to guide you into the truth.

It is not that the rabbis meant evil. They really believed in what they did, and there is often beauty and wisdom in their words. They were totally committed to their traditions, and through these traditions, they sought to bind the people of Israel together. But, while the traditions may have bound us together, they have, more importantly, bound us up. You can be free today.

"To the Jews who had believed Him, Jesus said, 'If you hold to My teaching, you are really My disciples. Then you will know the truth, and the truth will set you free'" (John 8:31-32).

Commentary by Sid Roth

I never heard much talk about the Messiah when I was a child. At our Passover seder we would open the door for Elijah to announce the Messiah. But the adults viewed the event as a fairy tale, almost like the Jewish version of Santa Claus. As I got older, I realized it was just "pretend," but I went along with the charade for the sake of the young children and "tradition."

Every Passover we read Psalm 118:22: "The stone which the builders rejected is become the chief cornerstone." Now I know that the cornerstone we builders (the Jewish people) rejected is the Messiah. No wonder Elijah never came to our Passover seder. Messiah had already come to die at Passover. Isaiah 53:7 says He was "like the [Passover] lamb which is led to the slaughter."

The name "Passover" comes from Exodus 12:13:

> *And the blood shall be to you for a token upon the houses where ye are; and when I see the blood, I*

will pass over you; and there shall be no plague against you to destroy....

But why was blood necessary? Leviticus 17:11 says,

For the life of the flesh is in the blood; and I have appointed it for you upon the altar to make an atonement for your souls; for the blood it is that maketh an atonement for the soul.

In other words, a blood sacrifice was the only acceptable substitute to atone for sin. During the first Passover, the blood was to be applied to the doorposts. Later, under the Mosaic Covenant, an animal had to be sacrificed in the Temple on the altar (see Lev. 1:11).

This is why we read in the Talmud, Yoma 5a, there can be no Yom Kippur without blood. Since the Temple was destroyed in A.D. 70, *there have been no Temple sacrifices for forgiveness of sin.*

In fact, *40 years before* the Temple was destroyed, the ancient rabbis recognized ominous supernatural signs that God no longer accepted the animal sacrifices that were offered (Yoma 39a,b). *That was the year Jesus died for our sins.*

Even the Jewish prophet Daniel said our Messiah would come and die, not for His own sins, but for ours *before* the Temple was destroyed (see Dan. 9:26).

True Judaism requires the blood of atonement of Jesus!

Since we have no Temple today, either our sins cannot be atoned for, or God has already sent His Messiah.

Of whom is this Yom Kippur prayer from a traditional Jewish prayer book speaking?

> Our righteous anointed is departed from us: horror hath seized us, and we have none to justify us. He hath borne the yoke of our iniquities and our transgression, and is wounded because of our transgression. He beareth our sins on His shoulder, that He may find pardon for our iniquities. We shall be healed by His wound, at the time that the Eternal will create Him as a new creature.[13]

Endnotes

1. H. Chaim Schimmel, *The Oral Law: A Study of the Rabbinic Contribution to Torah She-Be-Al-Peh*, rev. ed. (Jerusalem, New York, NY: Feldheim, 1987), italics added.

2. Z.H. Chajes, *The Student's Guide Through the Talmud*, trans. and ed. Jacob Schacter (New York, NY: Feldheim, 1960), 4.

3. See Nachmanides to Deuteronomy 17:11 and also the Babylonian Talmud, Baba Batra 12a.

4. See Maimonides' introduction to his commentary on the Mishnah.

5. See again Maimonides' introduction to his commentary on the Mishnah, and also the Babylonian Talmud, Yebamot 102a.

6. See the introduction to his *Ketzot HaHoshen* on *Hoshen Mishpat* in *Shulhan Arukh*.

7. Dr. J.H. Hertz, *The Pentateuch and Haftorahs* (London: Soncino, 1978), 316. The only real issue is whether to translate the Hebrew word *rabbîm* in this verse with "many" or "mighty." (The Talmudic passage in Baba Mesia 59b, of course, understood the word to mean "many"—in other words, the majority.) Either way, the meaning is impossible to dispute: *don't* follow the *rabbîm!*

8. See the Babylonian Talmud, Berakot 54a.

9. See, for example, the Jerusalem Talmud, Kiddushin
    1:2, 59d; the Babylonian Talmud, Sotah 16a, with
    Rashi's comments to the words '*oqeret* and *halakah.*

10. See also Gittin 60a in the Babylonian Talmud.

11. It is possible that a rabbinic Jew might point to
    Nehemiah 8:8, the only verse which mentions that the
    Levites made the Law clear as it was being read. This
    means either that they translated it into a more under-
    standable language (probably Aramaic for the exiles),
    or else they explained its meaning. This, of course, was
    the role of the priests and Levites: to educate the peo-
    ple in the Torah (see Leviticus 10:10-11). But, once
    again, to make some connection between this verse and
    an alleged unbroken chain of binding tradition is to
    build a mountain out of a non-existent mole hill. Also,
    the context makes it absolutely clear that the center of
    attention and authority was the written Word alone—as
    emphasized in the numerous verses just cited. The rest
    of Nehemiah 8 also shows us that the Jewish people
    then did what the Law literally told them to do, without
    any extra traditions or interpretations added on. And
    so, Nehemiah 8:15 says that the Jews followed what was
    written in Leviticus 23:37-40. They obviously had no
    clue that the Talmud would later claim that Leviticus 23
    could not be understood without all kinds of special
    interpretations and specific traditions.

12. See, for example, Leviticus 24:10-23; Numbers 9:1-14;
    15:32-36; 27:1-5; Zechariah 7.

13. *Form of Prayers for Day of Atonement,* rev. ed., (New York: Rosenbaum and Werbelowsky, 1890), 287-88.

CHAPTER 8
BY RANDY AND TRICIA HORNE

CHAPTER 8

It Was Not for Me

Tricia: Why did Jesus have to die for my sins? Raised as a Catholic, this concept was still foreign to me. Everyone knows if you're a good person, you'll go to Heaven when you die. So why did Jesus have to die? It seemed odd. It didn't fit the character of God—or did it? Since I had little knowledge of the Hebrew Scriptures, Jesus' death in exchange for our salvation didn't make much sense to me. But God was about to use a young Jewish man named Randy to draw me into a relationship with Him.

At the time I met Randy, I had been in a period of seeking God for answers. The two questions that bothered me most were: Why did I have terrible back pain? and Why didn't God answer my prayers to heal it? I would go to Mass, pray, pick up the missalette, and skip over all the traditional prayers just to get to God's Word. I knew the Scriptures were the real thing, what church should be all about. But I would kneel, stand, genuflect, bless myself, and do other religious things out of respect.

> **Little did I know that my mother (a quiet believer) had been listening regularly to a radio program called *Messianic Vision*.**

What did Randy have to do with all this? Little did I know that my mother (a quiet believer) had been listening regularly to a radio program called *Messianic Vision*. One day Sid Roth, the host of the program, said on the air, "The Jewish person that God has put in your life is no accident." My mother thought, *That's nice. But I don't know any Jewish people that well*. Within a matter of a few weeks, I told her I had met a nice Jewish guy. Immediately, she made the connection, but she told me nothing about it at the time. After we had been dating for seven or eight months, I told my mother I didn't know how we could pursue marriage with Randy being Jewish and me, Catholic. She suggested I check out the local Messianic Jewish congregation and start listening to Sid Roth's program. When she explained who Sid was, I thought, *A Jewish person who believes in Jesus. How unique*. But was it really? Paul, Peter, Matthew, Mark, John, Stephen—what were these men? Protestants? Catholics? Greek Orthodox? *No*. They were all *Jewish*. *OK*, I thought, *I'll tune in to this program on the way to work*. After all, this might be a compromise that would work for us. Maybe

Randy could be one of these Jewish people who believes in Jesus.

Jesus, You Loved Me That Much?

So I started listening to testimony after testimony of Jews and Gentiles touched by the powerful love of God. I would weep; I couldn't get enough. I was hungry for truth—for God. I sent for teaching tapes, testimonies, and Bibles. It was all so wonderful. I began to be convicted of sin in my life. The depth and weight of it was suddenly very heavy. I knew I needed pardoning; my sin was coming between me and God.

At the same time, I was listening to Sid and others explaining God's plan of salvation. From the very beginning, God required an atonement, a sacrifice for man's sins. Israel's sacrificial system in the Old Testament was a foreshadowing of Jesus atoning for my sins. Wow! No one is righteous, not one; all of us have gone astray, each one has turned to his own way, but God has laid the iniquity of all of us on Jesus (see Isa. 53:6). This is a better, more excellent way than the Temple sacrificial system because it brings us into a relationship with God.

> **This is a better, more excellent way than the Temple sacrificial system because it brings us into a relationship with God.**

Jesus, you loved me that much? I found myself crying out to God and asking Him for forgiveness one day in the car while tuned in to *Messianic Vision* on my way to work. So began my new life with God. I couldn't stop thinking about Him; I wanted all I could get. From religion I knew about Him and even believed in Him. But now I *knew Him*. What a difference!

In contrast, Randy didn't seem to care whether He even existed. Could we actually pursue marriage like this? Where should I go for advice?

The source who first shared the Gospel with me seemed like a good place to start. Being a new believer with a lot of chutzpah, I called Sid and told him my situation. He said, "No, you can't marry this man, but you can continue to pray that God will show him the truth." That answered that question.

What was God doing in Randy's life?

Randy: I was brought up in a reformed Jewish home. I went to Hebrew school three times a week for six years mainly to prepare for my bar mitzvah. Our family celebrated the high holy days out of tradition rather than out of Torah observance. I always wondered, *What is the sense of any of this?* I had the impression that most of the people present were there just because it was what Jewish people did on these holidays. Hebrew school was not something I enjoyed; for me it was a burden worse than public school because it cut into all of my after-school activities.

> **I don't remember a single time asking myself if I thought God existed or asking Him who He was.**

I should have been seeking answers to questions about who God was and how He related to my life. But I was so caught up in sports, who *I* was, where *I* was going, and how *I* would get there, that God never was an issue. I don't remember a single time asking myself if I thought God existed or asking Him who He was. My bar mitzvah was a fun time. I remember studying hard so as not to make a mistake. I got my wish and made it through without any flaws. Not making a mistake was much more important to me than the ceremony or any other part of my bar mitzvah. In my family, the bar mitzvah was the pinnacle of each child's Jewish studies. Once you went through this door, you no longer had to attend Hebrew school. As a family, we still attended high holiday services together, but for me it remained hollow and meaningless. The deepest questions I faced at that time were *Why am I at this service?* and *When can I leave?*

Someone Was Listening

That all changed in the summer after I graduated from college, while vacationing on Cape Cod. I met Tricia, whom God would use to change my life from shallowness to one of truly caring about people.

After months of trying to persuade Tricia to yield to my ways, I finally realized it was much easier to yield to hers. Though Tricia was a Catholic, the only thing this meant to me was that she went to church and I didn't. I had very little knowledge about her religion. At this point in my life, I did not attend any religious services other than the dinners my parents held at their house during the Jewish holidays. My understanding of God had not changed—He didn't bother me (or so I thought), and I didn't bother Him.

As Tricia and I started to get more serious about our relationship, religion became more of an issue. Instead of going out with my friends one Friday night, she suggested we attend a Messianic Jewish congregation. I wanted to refuse, but I didn't feel like fighting about it, so I agreed. The service was very Jewish, but different from anything I had experienced. I had never been exposed to individual and corporate spontaneous prayer. It was obvious as these people prayed that they knew someone was listening. The people were nice, but it was not for me.

> **It was obvious as these people prayed that they knew someone was listening.**

We did not return for five months. Neither of us had accepted Jesus as Lord and Savior at this point, although Tricia was truly searching. Then, in the summer of 1985, Tricia gave her life to the Lord. In September she asked me what I was doing for the high holidays. When I told her I didn't have plans since my family was celebrating in New

York with relatives, she suggested we go back to Ruach Israel to see what a Messianic service was like for the holidays. Once again, I agreed.

This time the service was not as foreign to me. Some parts were vaguely familiar, and I even remembered some of the chants. Tricia enjoyed the service so much she wanted us to start attending on a regular basis. We worked out a system where we would meet at a location halfway between our workplaces, park one of the cars, and take the other to the meeting on Friday nights. Many times I would try to convince her that after a long week of work we should skip the service and go somewhere to relax, but to no avail. She would reply, "You can do that, but I really want to attend the services."

After a few weeks of attending, I thought I might as well try and get something out of it, so I began to listen more attentively and even started to read the Bible. Before bed I would pray to God and ask Him to show Himself to me. Sometimes I would say "in Jesus' name" to see if anything would happen. As time went on, I learned more about God. But I still had no relationship with Him.

My Neck Has Been Healed!

Sid Roth came to speak at the Copley Place Hotel in Boston on Saturday, April 26, 1986. Tricia had been avidly listening to him on the radio and now of course wanted to attend his meeting. In my mind, we had already gone to service Friday night, and now she wanted to ruin Saturday too. I protested. She persisted.

We went to hear this man speak about how he came to know Jesus and how God had restored his mind and marriage. I thought this was interesting, but I had heard others say the same thing before on the tapes Tricia had been giving me. Near the end of the night, he called people forward who needed to be healed. Tricia went forward for her back, and I went with her. Standing next to Tricia at the front was a woman whom I had met earlier in the week at a Passover seder. I knew she did not believe in Jesus. I came to find out later that the only reason she was there was because it was her husband's birthday, and all he wanted was for her to come and hear Sid. This woman had been in a very serious car accident and could not move her neck. She wore a TENS unit hooked to her neck to stimulate nerve endings to help with the pain. Sid went down the line praying for people, and, of course, they were falling over just like you would see on television. When he got to this woman and Tricia, they didn't fall over, and then the next person in line did. I had it all figured out. He must be paying these people to fall over, and I knew Tricia and this woman were not part of it.

After Sid was finished praying, he said he felt that someone had been supernaturally healed, so he told the people to very slowly move the area in their body that needed healing to check it out. My eyes first went to Tricia. Then I saw the woman next to her shaking her neck and shouting, "My neck! My neck! I can move my neck!"

> **Although I did not understand
> what was happening, I knew I had
> encountered the presence of God,
> and my life would never be the same.**

At that point it almost seemed like I disappeared, because I started to weep—not just shed a tear, but really weep. Although I did not understand what was happening, I knew I had encountered the presence of God, and my life would never be the same.

The next morning I remember waking up and looking at the ceiling and thinking something was very different. Everything was the same, but the way I was looking at it was 180 degrees different from the way I had seen it a day earlier. I later asked Tricia what had happened to me the night before that could make such a difference. She stated calmly, "You had a born-again experience."

I started reading the Bible again and found that passages I couldn't understand before now made complete sense. I was a changed man. Jesus was for me!

Randy and Tricia were married on July 18, 1987, in a beautiful Messianic Jewish ceremony. They now have two children: Daniel Joseph, born July 4, 1990; and Joshua Michael, born November 21, 1993, and are raising them up to love and serve the Messiah of Israel. The Lord has significantly healed Tricia's back, and she leads a normal life free from the agony of back pain.

Commentary by Sid Roth

Randy and Tricia Horne are typical of the many couples who have intermarried. The Jewish community has done research predicting that if intermarriage and assimilation trends continue, there will be very few Jewish people left in America.

Not to worry. God says as long as this earth exists there will be physical Jews (see Jer. 31:35, verse 36 in some versions).

I see something far deeper in the union of Jew and Gentile in marriage. The one-flesh unity of Randy and Tricia reflects the shalom that will make us all one (Jew and Gentile) under the banner of Messiah's love. The rabbis say Jesus is the Messiah of the Gentiles, and we Jews are still waiting for our Messiah. Isaiah 11:10 says from the root of Jesse (David's father) will the Messiah come as a sign to the Gentiles (nations). In other words, the Gentiles will follow the Jewish Messiah.

We Jews believe in one God and one Messiah. Now if the rabbis say Jesus is the Gentile Messiah—by logic that makes Him the Jewish Messiah!

Besides, how can we have peace on earth unless the whole world follows the same Messiah?

Come quickly, Lord Jesus.

CHAPTER 9
BY BATYA SEGAL

CHAPTER 9

Bat Shalom: Daughter of Zion

At the beginning of this century rumors began to circulate that a Jewish State was about to be reborn in the land of our forefathers. Excitement swelled in the Jewish community in Yemen as they felt the days of the Messiah were soon to come. Many Jewish people started to make their way back to Zion. Leaving everything behind except their most essential belongings, they set out on the long perilous journey across the desert, some carrying their children on their shoulders. They had little food or drink. Many suffered from exhaustion, and many died—but they died full of hope and faith, knowing they were returning to the land of their forefathers.

In the late 1930s, my father left Yemen for Israel (then called Palestine), traveling by boat from Yemen to Egypt, and from there by train. Most of the family had died either in Yemen or on the way to Israel. Upon arrival in Israel my father joined his one surviving brother. About this same time, my mother and her family settled in Jerusalem.

> **After the rebirth of Israel, the new government committed itself to bringing back the Jewish people from all over the world.**

During the 1948 War of Independence, my father joined the Jewish forces fighting for the survival of the newly born Jewish State of Israel. He served in Ramat Rachel, a kibbutz just south of Jerusalem. After the rebirth of Israel, the new government committed itself to bringing back the Jewish people from all over the world. In 1950, an airlift called *Operation Magic Carpet* brought home to Israel a large part of the Yemenite Jewish community within a short period of time. Most of them had never even seen an airplane before. The rabbi explained from Isaiah 40:31 that God would lead them *"on wings like eagles,"* which dispersed any fears they may have had of flying, for they knew prophetically they were being taken home to be prepared for the days of redemption.

He Hears Your Prayers

The Israeli Yemenite Jewish community in which I was raised was Orthodox. My parents kept a kosher home and were strict observers of *Torah* (the five books of Moses). They kept the *Shabbat* (Sabbath) and all the feasts of Israel.

As I grew up, I went to an Orthodox girls' school in our neighborhood. Every morning we prayed as our forefathers had for two thousand years. At school we learned about the Messiah, who would come and redeem the Jewish people. He would reveal to the world that the God of Israel is the true God and would bring peace to all nations. He would sit on His throne in Jerusalem and rule the world with an iron rod. Though we learned this, the emphasis in our school was on the *Dinim*, the laws and commandments we had to follow as observant Jews. It was not a subject that excited us very much. I could not understand how it would bring me to a closer and deeper understanding of God, but I knew from studying the Jewish prophet, Isaiah, that God's thoughts were higher than my thoughts, so I didn't argue.

> **My father read his Bible every day when he returned from work. He instilled in me a love for and firm belief in God and His Word.**

The atmosphere at home was warm, loving, and full of music. When we came together with family and friends on Shabbat, holidays, and special occasions, we sang and prayed according to the Yemenite traditions.

My father read his Bible every day when he returned from work. He instilled in me a love for and firm belief in God and His Word. He taught me, "Never forget that God exists. Whenever you need Him, for whatever reason, then

He is always there to help you. Turn to God because He hears your prayers, and He knows your needs."

Every evening before I went to sleep, my father and I quoted together a passage of Scripture I knew by heart:

> *Sh'ma Yisrael, Adonai Elohenu, Adonai Echad.*
> *Ve-Ahavta Et Adonai Eloheicha Bechol Levavcha*
> *Uv'chol Nafshecha Uv'chol me-odech* …. *["Hear,*
> *O Israel: The Lord our God, the Lord is one. Love*
> *the Lord your God with all your heart, with all*
> *your soul, and with all your might …"]* (Deu-
> teronomy 6:4-9 NKJV).

I followed this with a personal talk with God. I used to bring before Him all the things of the day about which I was concerned, and I had the assurance that He heard my prayers and was meeting my needs. I knew God was my Father in Heaven, and I loved Him, but there were aspects of His character—His righteousness, holiness, and judgment—I did not understand, and so I feared Him as well.

As a child I loved art and got good grades in painting and drawing. I also was very interested in theatre and had the opportunity to act in some productions. I began to attend a children's group at the main radio station of Israel where we read stories and sketches on the radio. I loved it. This opened a whole new world for me. The director said I had an excellent voice for radio, and he could help me to make this my profession when I graduated.

My father would tell me, "Don't spread yourself so thin. Concentrate on one thing, and do it well." I knew this was very good advice, but I loved all I did, and it was difficult for me to give up anything.

I had the support and love of both my parents; my father, in particular, always encouraged and complimented me. Of course, the youngest child generally gets the most attention, so at times I was spoiled.

Miracle War

As I was preparing to finish elementary school and begin the summer holidays in June 1967, Israel suddenly found herself embroiled in what became known as the Six Day War. Israelis remember it as the "Miracle War." I was surprised to see that both of my brothers and my father were called to serve in the reserves. For seven days our family sat in the neighbor's basement, anxiously waiting to hear the news. Our only contact with the outside world was the radio. Every hour, when we heard the beep, we ran to listen to the latest bulletins.

> Israelis remember it as the "Miracle War." ...For seven days our family sat in the neighbor's basement, anxiously waiting to hear the news.

On the second day of the war, all the adults in the room began jumping with joy, hugging each other, and shouting. When I asked why, I was told that Jerusalem had been reunited, and our Israeli flag had been lifted on the

Temple Mount. Even as a child I realized this was a miracle only God could have performed. After two thousand years of foreign domination, Israel had expanded her borders to the heartland of her ancient territory! I began to understand God's prophetic word for the Jewish people.

I Need Freedom

When I was 12 years old and in a secondary school, I started to question my way of life. I began to break away from the teachings of my youth and go my own way. Since I greatly respected my parents and did not want to hurt them, I waited for the appropriate time and then explained my feelings to them. "I can't live this way anymore," I said. "I respect your lifestyle, but I need to explore a different one for me. I believe very strongly in God, but the *mitzvot* (laws) that I have been taught seem old-fashioned and not suitable for life today. I find I am unable to keep them with my whole heart, and I do not feel they bring me closer to God." I asked for their permission to go to a public high school.

My father has always been an open-minded man, so he said: "It is all right. You can do that as long as you are happy. But do not forget who your God is and where you come from."

And so I transferred to public school. This proved to be a great challenge. I was confronted with a totally different culture. And much to my surprise, some teachers, including the head teacher, did not believe in the Bible as the Word of God. Instead, they viewed the Bible as a collection of mythical tales not really inspired by God.

He singled out one boy in our class, who wore a *kippah*, as the object of sarcastic remarks and ridicule.

An even greater shock was finding that one of my teachers was an avowed atheist and particularly sharp toward any student who believed in God. He singled out one boy in our class, who wore a *kippah*, as the object of sarcastic remarks and ridicule.

My frustrations at this new school challenged me to study the Bible for myself. It was an eye-opening experience to study the books of Isaiah, Ezekiel, Jeremiah, and the other prophets. The prophecies concerning the return of the Jews to our homeland amazed me.

Because of my disenchantment over the way the Bible and other subjects were taught, I began to question the wisdom of attending public school. After two and one-half years, I left and enrolled in a school at which I could study mostly at home and go to classes just two days each week.

This was a period of deep soul-searching for me, a time of seeking for truth. Since I was studying at home, I had a lot of time to think and read. I knew I had not found satisfaction in a religious Orthodox lifestyle, even though I appreciated and identified with the traditions. But I had to ask myself, If keeping the commandments does not bring me peace and a closer relationship with God, then what does? I was searching for the answers to other questions as well: What is the purpose of my life here on earth? Who is God, really? What will happen to me after I die?

I tried to find answers in philosophical books, but they left me confused, raising more questions than answers. I gained no satisfaction from studying them.

Yom Kippur War

My quest for truth was suddenly interrupted by the Yom Kippur War in 1973. This was the hardest war Israel had ever faced. All our Arab neighbors attacked us, declaring a Holy War for Allah, on the holiest day of the Jewish year. Their sole intent was to destroy Israel and annihilate the Jewish population. We were totally unprepared, and consequently this war was a terrible tragedy for us. In Israel, in time of war, all reserve units are called up to strengthen the army. My two brothers and my father were again fighting in a war they had not wanted. Unlike 1967, this became a very personal war to me, as many of my friends and neighbors were either wounded or killed. I was devastated and in deep mourning. I cried to God for answers.

In January 1974, I began my military service, which every Israeli teenager enters at age 18. I served in the navy. It was just after the Yom Kippur War, and I saw some of my friends and acquaintances coming home wounded, some very severely, from the war. This increased my longing to know God and to know what the hereafter had in store for me. I asked all sorts of questions, but never received any clear answers.

Premature Marriage

I had served in the navy for one year when I married and obtained a release from service. A release was generally granted to girls getting married and starting a home. My husband, Avi, was an old friend I had known before I went into the navy. He was six years older than I and a confirmed atheist.

I still do not know what induced me to marry. As I reflect on it now, I realize I was far too young and made an impulsive decision. However, there was a lot of confusion in those days and emotions were blown out of proportion. I had lost friends in the war and felt I was in danger of losing another. Even though the marriage was a mistake, I know God was watching over my life.

Our relationship fell apart after only one year. After giving up all hope that our marriage would ever amount to anything, we agreed to separate. But the day we decided to get a divorce, Avi had to go to the Galilee on a press assignment (he was a press photographer). On the way back he was involved in a serious traffic accident in which his friend, the driver of the car, was killed, and Avi was seriously injured. It was a miracle he came out of the wreckage alive. He suffered a severe concussion, which the doctors told him would require a long period of rest. Ironically, just a few days after the accident, I discovered I was pregnant. Because of Avi's injuries and my pregnancy, we decided to stay together. When he left the hospital, however, Avi went to his mother's home for several months to recuperate.

Transcendental Meditation

Meanwhile, I was under tremendous pressure. I was 20 years old, pregnant with my first baby, and in a marriage hanging together by a thread. I was trying to earn a living and at the same time visit my husband in the hospital every day. I had to travel from Jerusalem to Tel Aviv, and then spend hours in the intensive care unit. Since I could not really communicate with Avi, I would sit and watch the injured soldiers entering the hospital. One had been explaining to his friends how to dismantle a hand grenade when it exploded in his face. His brain had died, but his heart kept beating. I saw others die or remain comatose.

> **I was under tremendous pressure.
> I was 20 years old, pregnant with
> my first baby, and in a marriage
> hanging together by a thread.**

Again I was caught in a web of circumstances that forced me to think about issues of life and death. I knew there had to be answers to my questions—answers that would change my life. I also knew I would have no peace until I found them.

I got a part-time job working for the Ministry of the Treasury. While there, I made friends with a lady deeply involved in transcendental meditation (TM). She knew I was going through a hard time and encouraged me to come to their meetings, believing they held the answer for me. In my desperation, I finally yielded to her persuasions and let her enroll me in a course. I had been very concerned this might be a religion, despite her assurance it wasn't. However, toward the end of the course, my friend said, "I forgot to tell you, there is a closing ceremony, but you can ignore what takes place." This aroused my curiosity.

We were told to bring an apple and a new white handkerchief as an offering for the maharishi (though I did not realize at first what was taking place). One by one we were taken into a small room with a TM instructor who stood in the back whispering incantations while the incense smoke arose by the picture of the guru. I laid down my apple as an offering to the maharishi. Then the instructor gave me my own special mantra to repeat while meditating.

The ceremony made me very uncomfortable, and I went home in despair. This was in stark contrast to TM's promises of personal fulfillment, joy, peace, and contentment. I tried to ignore the religious part of the course and continued doing the exercises and the early morning meditations as I believed it would help me in my pregnancy.

> **Then suddenly it hit me: "By doing TM, I'm worshiping other gods!"**

I knew something was wrong, but I could not put my finger on it. Then suddenly it hit me: "By doing TM, I'm worshiping other gods!" Once I understood the implications, I was almost physically sick. I confronted my TM friend: "You said this wasn't a religious course, but now I realize I was ensnared in idolatry!"

A New Profession

As time went by, Avi improved physically. He started working a few hours a day in his lab, but was frustrated with his physical limitations and inability to provide properly for his family. He became self-absorbed and lost his temper easily. It was difficult to communicate with him. After the dreadful experience of TM and with my married life deteriorating, I turned more and more to God with my questions, crying out to Him for comfort, appealing to Him for help in my distress, and begging Him to reveal Himself to me.

> **After the dreadful experience of TM and with my married life deteriorating, I turned more and more to God with my questions, crying out to Him for comfort, appealing to Him for help in my distress, and begging Him to reveal Himself to me.**

When trouble comes, it does not seem to stop. Avi broke the metal plate in his hip and had to be rushed to the hospital. He had an emergency operation and once again was confined to the hospital for several months. This time he had a plaster body cast. He was admitted to a private hospital close to home, so I didn't have to travel as far to visit him.

Through Avi's long-term illness, I had taken on the responsibility of supporting the family, but I was only working part-time at the Ministry of Treasury, so I began to look for a second job.

It was at that time that God began to answer my prayers. A friend of ours knew of a printing business looking for a computer typist to operate a typesetting machine. One day he called us to see how we were doing. He asked if I knew of anyone looking for a part-time job. "Yes, I know someone— me," I said. "But I have no training in typesetting."

He quickly replied, "That doesn't matter. If you take the job, they will train you!"

"Then I'll take it," I announced. "I would love to learn a new profession." Little did I know what God had in mind.

From my first day at the printing firm, I knew I was part of something very special. There was a wonderful atmosphere, and the few people I saw were very kind to me. Even the interview with the manager was pleasant.

Although I started out with no knowledge of computers, after a while I became quite proficient. I worked in a tiny room where I operated one computer and Ibrahim, a young Beduin Arab, operated the other. He was about my age, 23, married, and already had four children.

A Different New Testament

One morning my employer handed me an envelope with a manuscript for me to typeset. When I pulled it out, I discovered it was the New Testament in Hebrew. My first reaction was, "Oh no, this can't be real! What sort of place is this? Why do they want to print the New Testament in Hebrew here? Are they missionaries?"

For a while I sat there struggling with my conscience: *What* chutzpah *(nerve) they have! Shall I do it? What am I supposed to do?* My mind whirled. I needed the job, but how could I work on such a thing? I felt I had no choice, so I began. It was difficult to open the manuscript and start typing, thinking I was contributing to the work of missionaries, helping them convert Jewish people and steal Jewish souls. I vividly recalled a story I had read as a child about a widow named Hannah who had seven children. She lived during the time of the Inquisition. When faced with the choice of death or bowing to the cross, she heroically refused to yield, choosing death rather than conversion.

> **The longer I worked on the manuscript, the clearer it became to me the New Testament was a Jewish book!**

As I began to type and read the New Testament, it was different than I had expected. To my amazement, on the first page was the genealogy of Yeshua, which showed Him to be a descendant of Abraham of the line of David. My first discovery was that Yeshua was a Jew! And the disciples were Jews! The longer I worked on the manuscript, the clearer it became to me the New Testament was a Jewish book! Then the questions began. *What's wrong with it?* I thought. *Why are the rabbis so against it? Why do they reject this book?* All these questions went through my mind while typing.

I had been brought up to believe that Jesus was the God of the Christians and that the New Testament was a Christian book, yet I knew I was typesetting a book that was completely Jewish. How could this be? And if Christians followed a Jewish book, how could they have persecuted the Jewish people for so many centuries? And so the struggle for my salvation began. My heart was no longer at peace. In my head it made sense to me that Yeshua was the Jewish Messiah, but my upbringing kept my heart from accepting that idea. As I read the words of Yeshua in *HaBrit HaHadashah* (the New Testament), truth began to shine into my life. Yeshua said all actions stem from a person's heart, and God is concerned with our thoughts and motives—not just our actions. That really struck home.

> **Then came the amazing revelation of eternal life. I thought, *This is the answer I have been seeking for a long, long time.* ... The words of Yeshua pierced to the very depths of my heart, and although I was still fighting, God was winning the battle.**

Then came the amazing revelation of eternal life. I thought, *This is the answer I have been seeking for a long, long time. All I have known up until now has been very obscure concerning eternal life, but Yeshua's words are very clear and certain, and I can understand them.* The words of Yeshua pierced to the very depths of my heart, and although I was still fighting, God was winning the battle.

Is This Truth?

Two major questions remained: Is this really the truth, or am I deceiving myself? and Why does the name of Yeshua generate so much anger among the Orthodox Jews?

I began to look up the references in the *Tanakh* (the Old Testament) to check them against quotations in the Gospels. I wanted to know if the prophecies and promises of Yeshua's coming were really written in the Tanakh. I delved deeply into the subject.

After many months of searching, I felt I could go no further without help. So I began to ask all my friends, "Who is the Messiah really?" "Why hasn't the Messiah come yet?" "Why couldn't Yeshua be the Messiah?" I bombarded everyone I met with my questions, even people I hardly knew. I was not ashamed, but was very open about it.

Still I had doubts about whether Yeshua was Messiah. Sometimes I felt as if I had found a great treasure, but a little later, I would dismiss it again. My turmoil lasted for months.

During this time, Avi was discharged from the hospital and came back to live with me again as we had decided to give our marriage another chance. While he had almost recovered from his initial concussion, his legs were still in casts.

After I had finished typing the New Testament, I was given various Christian books to typeset in Hebrew. These included *The Hiding Place,* a book about Corrie ten Boom, a Christian who had hidden Jews during the Holocaust; *Run Baby Run,* the story of Nicky Cruz, a New York gang leader whose life was changed by faith in Yeshua; and *Joni,* the story of Joni Erikson, whose faith had sustained her when she became a quadriplegic as the result of a swimming accident. Those books made a great impression on me. While I was working on the computer, tears would sometimes run down my cheeks. I saw how God's love had touched people and radically changed their lives.

I See an Angel

About nine months after I had started typesetting the New Testament and the other books into Hebrew, I was troubled more than ever with my many questions. But no one I asked was able to give me satisfactory answers.

One night in desperation I went to my bedroom and cried out to God: "God, please show me the way I should go. Is Yeshua the true Messiah of Israel, or is He a false Messiah? If He is the true Messiah, I want to follow Him and serve Him. But if He is not, please let me forget about Him."

Right after I prayed, I saw a vision of a man clothed in a long white robe. His bearded face was shining and full of glory. The countenance of the man was majestic. I did not understand the meaning of this vision, yet I felt God was trying to give me a sign.

> **"God, please show me the way I
> should go. Is Yeshua the true
> Messiah of Israel, or is He a false
> Messiah? If He is the true
> Messiah, I want to follow Him
> and serve Him. But if He is not,
> please let me forget about Him."**

The next day I left work at 3:00 P.M. and was standing at the bus stop watching for the next bus. Suddenly, I saw a man coming toward me from the other side of the street. I realized I had seen him before. He had the same face, the same long hair, the same beard, and the same clothes as the man I had seen in the vision the night before. A shock ran through my body, and the experience gave me goose bumps. I looked around to see if anyone else at the bus stop saw him, but no one indicated noticing him. As I looked back toward him, I saw that he had disappeared.

I realized this was God's sign. The tall, bearded man was the man in my vision. It couldn't be a coincidence, my meeting the same man from the vision in the street. I knew it was an angel, and I rejoiced!

At last I was convinced Yeshua was the Messiah. I had total peace and an overwhelming joy in my heart. The struggles between my head and my heart were over. I was thrilled to know I was finally on the right path. This was my turning point.

> At last I was convinced
> Yeshua was the Messiah.
> I had total peace and an
> overwhelming joy in my heart.

When I got home, I was so excited about what I had seen, I blurted out to my husband, "Do you know what has just happened? I had a vision, and after that I saw an angel, and he was from God. Yeshua is the Messiah. I'm certain of it!" The revelation was so real to me; I did not consider anyone might doubt it. But Avi, a confirmed atheist, looked at me mockingly as if I had gone crazy. He made fun of me in front of my friends. When he had an attentive audience, he would say sarcastically, "Have you heard? Batya saw an angel, and now she believes in Yeshu!" (This is a derogatory name for Yeshua.) On those occasions I wished the ground would swallow me.

When we were alone I would say to him, "You just don't do that sort of thing! This is something personal, something intimate. You can't ridicule prayer and the things that I experienced with God. This is something between me and God."

I Lose My Daughter

Our relationship continued to deteriorate. I was very vulnerable as a new believer in Yeshua. I had no idea what direction my life would take nor much inner certainty about the future. I needed brothers and sisters in the Body of Messiah to support me. But Avi forbade me to meet with other believers or to read the Bible.

"If you continue doing this," he told me, "I shall fight you in the highest courts and take our daughter away from you."

True to his word, Avi moved ahead with his vendetta. I was ordered to appear before the Rabbinical Court. When Avi arrived, I noticed he was carrying a briefcase. I had no idea what was in it. My lawyer, a religious man, could not guess either. When he came before the judge, Avi opened the case and produced all the books I had typed, plus my New Testament.

"These are her books," he shouted, pointing at me.

"She is a missionary! And I won't have her bringing up my daughter!" There was a great commotion in the court-room. The rabbis seemed gravely concerned.

After consultation, they forbade Avi to allow me into the house and said that I could no longer raise my daugh-ter. They gave him full custody. My lawyer requested a recess, but they refused. I shouted at the rabbis before I left the courtroom, "God is the only Judge. He will make the decision about where my daughter will be. If God wishes for her to be with me, He will make it possible." My courage to speak amazed me. I almost felt as though the Lord had spo-ken those words through me.

> **I hugged and kissed my daughter good-bye and closed the door of my house behind me. I had been banished.**

With a heavy heart and tears streaming down my face, I hugged and kissed my daughter good-bye and closed the door of my house behind me. I had been banished. Defeated. I couldn't understand why God had allowed it to happen.

Yeshua, Please Help!

"Lord," I cried, "this is too much for me. Please help me! I cannot bear this!" With my mouth I said that I was sacrificing my Isaac as Abraham had, but my heart was not in it. She was my daughter! I was leaving my daughter! It felt as though a sword were piercing my soul. I cried, "Oh, Yeshua, please help me!" Amazingly, the separation from my daughter lasted only three days. A finding by the civil court annulled the verdict of the religious court because of a technical error. But I knew it was a miracle from God.

My daughter was with me again! I could take her in my arms and hold her. By the grace of God, I have been able to bring her up, and she is still living with me to this very day. She is now 18 years old and about to enter the Israeli Army. I am proud of her and love her very, very much. The battle in the courts for custody of Tali lasted eight years, including about four years in the Supreme Court of Israel. Year after year it dragged on until Avi decided to marry another woman and pressed me to agree to a divorce.

> **It is amazing how God can use the evil things in the world to bring about good.**

It is amazing how God can use the evil things in the world to bring about good. This fight, which was really persecution for my belief in Yeshua, stimulated my spiritual growth. I had to learn to fight to survive, even though still a baby spiritually. The fight strengthened me, and the problems refined me. The Lord gave me many insights, and my relationship with Him became very deep and secure.

A few years later I became involved with a group of believers who were musicians; we would meet to sing and pray. One evening, we were praying together in a circle, and when I opened my eyes, I saw a young man who had come in late. There was something very familiar about him, though I had never met him before. After that, I kept running into him in Jerusalem. I learned that his name was Barry, and I found that I enjoyed his sense of humor. Barry's whole life before he came to the Lord had revolved around music. He once had been a professional rhythm and blues musician, a style of music totally alien to me. I had heard such music one time as a child, but did not like it at all. When Barry found Yeshua he gave up his guitar (although later God was to use this talent in ministry for Himself). Barry was one of the best guitarists I had ever heard, and, as I also played guitar, we really got on well together.

As the years went by, Barry and I got to know each other well. He was a constant prayer companion for me in my court battles over Tali. We began to work together and finally came to realize that God had brought us together to be man and wife. We had two wedding celebrations, a traditional Yemenite Jewish wedding and a Messianic celebration. It was a wonderful time for both of us. It was not easy for our parents to accept our faith, but the wedding helped give them some insight, and praise God, they never cut us out of their lives. Barry's father, a traditional, Conservative Jew, does not agree with the ultra-Orthodox position that Messianic Jews are no longer Jews.

My parents know I am a believer in Yeshua, and they accept it. They love Barry, and I am still my father's little girl. They love our children: our daughter Tali, our lovely six-year-old son, Ariel ("Lion of God" and one of the names of Jerusalem), and our beautiful daughter, Liran, who is almost two. My parents get great joy from their grandchildren. We have spent many a Shabbat at their table—a mixture of Yemenite Orthodoxy and Messianic Judaism. As Jewish Orthodox people who have great respect for God and His Word, they express their joy at seeing how God has blessed me with a new family.

Commentary by Sid Roth

The "Lubavitchers" are a sect within traditional Judaism. Many believe their rabbi, Manachem M. Schneersohn, who died in 1994, is the Messiah. This group has a synagogue in Siberia.

The president of this synagogue recently visited a local church in his area because he was friends with the pastor. At this meeting there was a Messianic Jewish dance group comprised of Jews, Gentiles, men, women, African American, white, and Hispanic dancers that touched the synagogue leader deeply. Afterward, he said, "Our traditional worship is dead. Many of our young people are leaving the synagogue. But I feel such joy and life in your worship. I feel God's presence. We want what you have. What is the difference between us?"

The leader of the dance group said, "There is only one difference. Our Messiah is Jesus. He died and rose from the dead 2,000 years ago. Your Messiah is Rabbi Schneerson, whom you expect to rise from the dead. But he has been dead for years and will never come back. What you are experiencing from our dance group comes from their intimacy with God. Without Messiah Jesus it is impossible to have intimacy with God."

After we Jewish people have intimacy with God, then our assignment is to tell Gentiles about the Jewish Messiah. Isaiah says the call of the Jew is to be "a light to the Gentiles [nations]" (Isa. 49:6 NKJV). The assignment of the Gentile believer in Jesus is to tell Jewish people about the Messiah (see Rom. 11:11). And when we all do our job, Messiah will return and usher in an age of peace.

CHAPTER 10

BY MANNY AND SANDRA SHESKIN BROTMAN

CHAPTER 10

The Amazing Jewish Book and the God-Shaped Hole in My Soul

And ye shall seek Me, and find Me, when ye shall search for Me with all your heart (Jeremiah 29:13).

One does not have to live too many years before discovering that there exists within a certain emptiness, a void or vacuum that the things of this world can never fill. Neither money nor sex, travel, fame, drugs, titles, possessions, nor any other human accomplishment can fill this emptiness.

I call this vacuum, "the God-shaped hole in my soul." I eventually discovered that this particular void is reserved only for the Creator of the Universe, the God of Abraham, Isaac, and Jacob Himself—to live in each of us personally.

Here, then, is the story of my personal search through religion, academics, sports, business, and the media; my discovery of the Bible—the amazing Jewish book; my coming to understand how to have a personal relationship with God; and my experiencing His abundant life.

I tried *religion*. I had a wonderful religion—Judaism. Both of my parents were Jewish. I attended a Conservative synagogue. I was born a Jew, and I would die a Jew! But somehow, even in the synagogue, the God of Abraham, Isaac, and Jacob seemed to be so far away. I didn't feel that I could live my whole life for only religion.

I tried *academics*. I had honors in scholarship both in high school and college. But I could not live my life only for a string of doctorate degrees after my name.

I excelled in *sports*. In Philadelphia, I was quarterback of the championship high school football team and pitcher for the winning city baseball team. I had awards in basketball and table tennis. But I couldn't live only for athletic accomplishments and the friends they brought.

I tried the *business* world. I worked my way up from production control, to vice president's assistant, and, eventually, to corporate president. I had a lovely ranch home in a modern Jewish community. Our company had a twin-engine aircraft and a pilot who flew me and the executives who worked for me wherever we wanted to go. But still, I couldn't live my life only for business accomplishments.

And, then, I experienced the *media*. I was Chairman of the Board of Fourth Television Network. We provided programming to 500 cable franchises. For a number of years, I produced and hosted a nationally syndicated daily radio show which aired on 22 stations. I have been interviewed on numerous national television and radio programs across the United States, Canada, and the Middle East, which were broadcast to millions of people. But even being involved with the media could not be the ultimate purpose of my life. There had to be something more.

During the course of my lifetime, I have been privileged to experience many things that other people would like to experience and have not been able to. But none of my accomplishments could ever fill that God-shaped hole within me. One day at the Fairmount Park Recreation Center in Philadelphia (before I had experienced most of the things described above), I met George Gruen, a Jewish Bible believer. George and his wife, Doris, lived their lives on a higher plane than anyone I had ever met. They had true joy, peace, happiness, and a genuine love for me and others. I wondered what made these people so different.

> **There had to be something more.**

George was a coach of baseball and basketball teams. Since I loved sports so much, I wanted to participate. Along with the competition, George conducted Bible studies from the Jewish Scriptures for all participating team members. For the first time in my life, I seriously considered the credentials and the message of the Jewish Bible.

The Credentials of the Amazing Jewish Bible

> *Wherewithal shall a young man cleanse his way?*
> *by taking heed thereto according to Thy Word....*
> *Thy Word have I hid in mine heart, that I might*
> *not sin against Thee* (Psalm 119:9,11).

First of all, I discovered that the Jewish Bible is historically accurate when checked against other existing historical records. And, in some cases, it gives the only sensible account for certain periods of time when no other historical records are available.

Then the Jewish Scriptures are geographically reliable and have been confirmed many times over by archaeologists who use the Bible as a "road map" to locate buried cities and historical artifacts. Israeli military leaders sometimes use ancient battle routes and follow battle strategies found in the *Tanakh* (Jewish Scriptures) in modern-day warfare against Israel's enemies.

> **Most amazingly, the Jewish Bible**
> **specifically foretold the future with**
> **100 percent accuracy in every instance.**

Most amazingly, the Jewish Bible specifically foretold the future with 100 percent accuracy in every instance. The Hebrew Scriptures prophesied of:

1) The Re-establishment of the State of Israel

In Isaiah 11:12, God said,

> *And He shall set up an ensign for the nations,*
> *and shall assemble the outcasts of Israel, and*
> *gather together the dispersed of Judah from the*
> *four corners of the earth.*

God said that He would make Israel like an "ensign" (in Hebrew, "a miraculous flag or banner") for the world to see. He would then re-gather the Jewish people from the four corners of the earth after almost 2,000 years of world-wide dispersion.

On May 14, 1948, Prime Minister David Ben-Gurion stood in Tel Aviv's Museum Hall and proclaimed the Statehood of Israel. A nation was born in a single day exactly as the Bible prophesied over 2,700 years ago (see Isa. 66:8)!

2) The Restoration of Hebrew, "The Pure Language"

In Zephaniah 3:9, it is written,

> *For then will I turn to the people a pure language,*
> *that they may all call upon the name of the Lord,*
> *to serve Him with one consent.*

Israel is a "melting pot" of Jewish people from more than a hundred nations of the world; yet, they all learn to speak biblical Hebrew with modern Hebrew words added. One may wonder why Hebrew is called a "pure" language in the Bible. That is because there are no words of vulgarity or profanity in biblical Hebrew!

Never before in the history of mankind has an ancient people been scattered across the face of the earth for almost 2,000 years and later restored to their own land with their own ancient national language. How did the Jewish prophet Zephaniah know that would happen?

3) The Miraculous Defeat of Israel's Enemies in Four Major Wars

Isaiah 19:16-17 predicts the miraculous victories of modern Israel over her enemies, which occurred in 1948 (War of Independence), 1956 (Sinai War), 1967 (Six Day War), and 1973 (Yom Kippur War):

> *In that day shall Egypt be like unto women: and it shall be afraid and fear because of the shaking of the hand of the Lord of hosts …. And the land of Judah shall be a terror unto Egypt … because of the counsel of the Lord of hosts, which He hath determined against it.*

During the four major wars, Israel's small population of several million Jews had to defend itself time after time against the growing Arab League of 20 nations (now 21 nations) with a population at that time of approximately 140 million Arabs. Israel was outnumbered *5 to 1 in soldiers, 3 to 1 in enemy aircraft and tanks, 8 to 1 in artillery, and 18 to 1 in missiles.* Israel's military budget paled to insignificance when contrasted against the tens of billions of petro-dollars Israel's enemies spent for Israel's destruction. And yet, Israel, even though out-manned, out-gunned, and out-financed, has won war after war against insurmountable odds. *There is no answer but God Himself, who foretold in the Bible this would happen.*

Here are three brief examples of the exciting miracles God performed on behalf of Israel:

A Jewish tour guide testified:

During the war, my men and I were trapped in a minefield. The mines started blowing up all around us. All of a sudden, a little whirlwind of sand appeared and led me and my men through the minefield to safety!

An Israeli wrote me:

I was down in the battlefield and saw on the hilltop a man completely dressed in white helping our soldiers from foxhole to foxhole. Whenever the man lifted his arms up toward heaven, the battle always went in the favor of our Israeli troops. I gave my binoculars to my General to get a better look. He, too, saw the man in white, who then disappeared in front of our eyes!

A reporter told me that his father (also a reporter) was on the Golan Heights after the Israelis captured it. His father asked the Syrian soldiers, "Why did you retreat from the few Jewish soldiers that first came up?" They replied, "You must be mistaken! We did not see a *few* Jewish soldiers. We saw *hundreds* of them!" Whom did these Syrian soldiers see? Did they see the angels of God? Could it be that once again God is sending His angels to fight for His Jewish people and putting a fear in the hearts of Israel's enemies according to Isaiah's prophecy?

4) Agricultural Miracles Would Occur When the Jews Returned to Israel

In Isaiah 35:1, it says,

The wilderness and the solitary place shall be glad for them; and the desert shall rejoice, and blossom as the rose.

When the Jewish people returned to Israel from the four corners of the earth, they found malaria-ridden swamps and parched, barren deserts. The nomads who occupied the land for centuries were not the "children" of the deserts; rather, they were the "fathers" of it. They contributed nothing to restore the land; through their negligence, it had gotten worse. When the Jews returned to their homeland, an agricultural transformation began to take place as prophesied by Isaiah.

When I lived in Chicago, I was able to buy luscious oranges from Israel. In Miami, I could buy tomato juice from Tel Aviv. And, now, in the Washington, D.C. area where I live, I can purchase beautiful fresh-cut flowers from Israel. One only has to visit the famous Carmel Market in Tel Aviv to see the fantastically huge citrus and produce that Israel grows.

The Scripture says, "the desert shall...blossom as the rose." The most important cut flowers that are exported from Israel are roses! The tiny nation of Israel is number three in the world for exporting cut flowers—valued at $140 million a year—with the majority going to Europe. How's that for a dry, parched, barren desert? Bananas, a *warm* climate fruit, are grown in the Jordan Valley with excellent results, while just five miles away, apples, a *cold* climate fruit, also yield a top-quality crop. I have witnessed this marvel with my own eyes.

In the short existence of modern-day Israel, it is already part of a select group of nations that not only produces enough food for its own citizens, but exports 20 percent of its total agricultural products to other countries of the world! Israel also exports its agricultural technology and "know-how" to third-world countries as well as to highly developed countries in Europe and to the United States.

Israel is the most water-efficient country in the world, regulating and controlling alternative water resources such as recycled water from industry and sewage from the domestic sector! Using integrated computerized control of irrigation and fertilization systems in a substantial percentage of Israeli field crops and horticulture minimizes labor costs and maximizes the best possible conditions for the crops. In a special station in Israel's Negev Desert, using desert methods and techniques of irrigation, *salty water* is pumped from the depths of the Negev with unsurpassed results in producing the best tasting and highest quality tomatoes to be found anywhere! Eggplant, yellow melons, potatoes, pears, and table grapes are also watered with this salty water and harvested in the Negev Desert. Once our Jewish people returned to the land, Isaiah's prophecies about flowers in the desert and Israel's agriculture proved to be right on target!

5) Israel's Waste Cities Would Be Rebuilt

The prophet Amos wrote in Amos 9:14,

> *And I will bring again the captivity of My people of Israel, and they shall build the waste cities, and inhabit them; and they shall plant vineyards,*

and drink the wine thereof; they shall also make
gardens, and eat the fruit of them.

Since 1948, the Jews have built their nation with one hand and with the other have held their weapons! Despite defending itself in four major wars; caring for the transportation, housing, language-training, employment, and education of millions of immigrants from over a hundred nations; forming a government; and developing an infrastructure, Israel has managed to build and finance a modern nation of which it can be proud!

What once were "waste cities" are now expanding modern cities and ports such as Jerusalem, Tel Aviv, Jaffa, Haifa, and many others. Since its independence, Israel has had a non-stop building program and is reclaiming the desert at such a rate that its map-makers have a hard time staying current. Israel has not only excelled in agriculture, but also in its technology, universities, sciences, defense, medicine, resorts, and much more. The State of Israel is exactly what the Bible said it would be!

6) The Jews Would Return to Israel From the Land of the North (Russia)

Jeremiah 16:14-15 and 23:7-8 tell about Exodus 2:

Therefore, behold, the days come, saith the Lord,
that it shall no more be said, the Lord liveth, that
brought up the children of Israel out of the land
of Egypt; but, the Lord liveth, that brought up the
children of Israel from the land of the north ....

If you were to fly north from Jerusalem, you would eventually come to Moscow. The former Soviet Union (especially Russia) contains the only sizable Jewish population north of Israel that could fit this prophecy. It is estimated that there are from two and one-half million (pure-blooded Jews) to ten million (intermarried and "closet" Jews) in the former USSR.

Whatever the numbers, well over a million Russian Jews have already immigrated to Israel in recent years. The majority of these immigrants are highly trained educators, physicians, engineers, and musicians who are infusing Israel with a windfall of intelligent professionals "from the land of the North," exactly as the Jewish Scriptures predicted over 2,600 years ago!

Is it any wonder I call it "The Amazing Jewish Bible?" If one ancient prophecy from the Jewish Scriptures came true, we could call it "luck." If two prophecies came true, we could call it "a lucky coincidence." If three prophecies came true, we could say "what a remarkable lucky coincidence!" But, when prophecy after prophecy after prophecy comes true specifically, by the sheer law of compound probabilities, we have passed from the realms of luck and coincidence, and God has given us a sure word of prophecy that we can live by and upon which we can base our decisions!

I and millions of others have concluded that the Jewish Bible is the most corroborated, authenticated document in the world. Yes, the Bible is confirmed by history, archaeology, geography, prophecy, and the Dead Sea Scrolls. And, most of all, it works in the lives of those who sincerely put it to the test. I can verify this by my own experience. This kind of evidence does demand a verdict. What should we do about it?

I thought it was fascinating, all those years ago, that God fulfilled Bible prophecy, but I wanted to know how that related to me. What was God's plan for me personally?

The Message of the Jewish Bible

> Come now, and let us reason together, saith the
> Lord: though your sins be as scarlet, they shall be
> as white as snow; though they be red like crimson,
> they shall be as wool (Isaiah 1:18).

As I searched the Jewish Scriptures, I discovered that God's plan to have my sins forgiven and to have me enter into a personal relationship with Him could be summarized in five spiritual principles. I call these "The Five Jewish Laws." In other words, just as the Creator has well-defined physical laws (such as gravity, centrifugal force, and inertia) that govern the operation of the universe, so He has well-defined spiritual laws that govern our relationship with Him. Here are these laws:

Law 1 Tells of God's *Purpose* ...

> ...*God created you and me to have a personal
> relationship with Himself, and, as a result of that
> relationship, to enjoy His abundant life!*

Nothing gives God greater pleasure than when you and I choose to have a personal relationship with Him out of our own free will!

> *The Lord hath made all things for Himself [His own pleasure]...* (Proverbs 16:4).

A personal relationship with God will bring you His abundant life of peace, purpose, meaning, joy, and happiness.

> *At thy right hand there are pleasures for evermore* (Psalm 16:11).

This is a wonderful life to have, isn't it? But most people don't seem to be experiencing this abundant life today. Why not? This brings us to Law 2.

Law 2 Reveals Man's *Problem* ...

> *...Sin separates you from a personal relationship with God and His abundant life. Sin also causes spiritual death.*
>
> *But your iniquities [your sins] have separated between you and your God ...* (Isaiah 59:2).
>
> *The soul that sinneth, it shall die [spiritual death]* (Ezekiel 18:4).

Sin also causes guilt, unhappiness, lack of peace, frustration, and a lack of purpose. *What is sin? It is the transgression or breaking of God's law.* Part of the *Shema* (Deuteronomy 6:5) says,

> *And thou shalt love the Lord thy God with all thine heart, and with all thy soul, and with all thy might.*

If we do not love God with all of our heart, soul, and might, then we have broken the most important and First Commandment and have sinned. If we put anything before God such as self, material possessions, sex, money, drugs, or anything else, then we have made idols of those things and have committed idolatry. If we hate somebody in our hearts, then we are murderers. If we lust in our hearts, then we are adulterers. If we steal, kill, lie, covet, work on the Sabbath, or dishonor our parents, then we have broken the Ten Commandments. Actually, our rabbis and scholars tell us that there are 613 Commandments in the Tenach that we should all keep.

> ## Who can keep all of these commandments? None of us!

Who can keep all of these commandments? None of us! First Kings 8:46 says,

> *For there is no man that sinneth not ....*

As I studied the Jewish Scriptures, I realized that, both knowingly and unknowingly, I had broken countless commandments of God and that I had to turn from these sins with God's help. Ezekiel 33:11 quotes the Lord God:

> *As I live, saith the Lord God, I have no pleasure in the death of the wicked [unforgiven]; but that the wicked [unforgiven] turn from his way and live: turn ye, turn ye from your evil [sinful] ways; for why will ye die, O house of Israel?*

I realized that I had sinned and needed God's help.

Are you willing to admit that you too have sinned and need God's help? That brings us to Law 3.

Law 3 Explains God's *Plan*...

A) You Cannot Remove Sin by Your Own Human Efforts.

None of us can get to Heaven by keeping the Ten Commandments (the law). The knowledge of sin is produced by God's law, which is so pure and perfect that it is His ruler or measurement to show us, as human beings, how far short we fall of God's glory and holiness. Without the law, we would not even know how sinful we are.

Man's plan is to try to remove his own sins by his own human efforts. These efforts may include religion (man's attempts to reach God) or just plain being "a do-gooder," hoping that one's good deeds outweigh one's bad deeds to attain self-righteousness. In Proverbs 14:12, it says,

> *There is a way which seemeth right unto a man,*
> *but the end thereof are the ways of death [spiritual*
> *separation from God]!*

Again, the Creator who has put a hundred billion galaxies in space in perfect mathematical and chronological precision is not sloppy when it comes to His spiritual laws. If one does not obey God's precise spiritual laws as revealed and confirmed in His Word, one cannot achieve God's required righteousness (right standing with God).

B) Sin Can Only Be Removed by Faith—Believing What God Says and Acting Upon it.

Righteousness comes by faith. Genesis 15:6 says,

> And he [Abraham, the Father of the Jewish
> People] believed [had faith] in the Lord; and He
> [God] counted it [Abraham's faith] to him for
> righteousness.

Righteousness with God does not come by our good works (*mitzvot*). For by God's grace—something that we don't deserve—you and I are forgiven through faith. It is not of ourselves. It is the gift of God, not of our human works, unless any of us should boast and say that we deserve it (see Eph. 2:8-9).

C) Faith Must Be Placed in God's Provided Blood of Atonement ("Covering" for Sin).

If one has spiritual faith in the sense that the Bible describes, then God requires an act of faith acceptable to Him. Leviticus 17:11 says,

> For it is the blood that maketh an atonement [cov-
> ering] for the soul.

When the Temple was in existence and the lamb was sacrificed on the altar providing the blood of atonement, this was an act of faith acceptable to God! But, since the Temple is no longer in existence, and the sacrificial system has ceased, how can we have the blood of atonement today by an act of faith? That brings us to Law 4.

Law 4 Shows God's *Provision*...

God has provided the blood of atonement today through a Perfect Sacrifice, One whom the Jewish Bible calls "The Messiah." The word *Messiah* means "The Anointed One."

Isaiah 53:5-6 says:

> *But He was wounded through our transgressions [rebellions], bruised through our iniquities [moral evils]: the chastisement [punishment] of our peace [welfare] was upon Him; and with His wounds [stripes, blood] we are healed [atoned for]. All we like sheep have gone astray [sinned]; we have turned every one to his own way; and the Lord hath caused the iniquity of us all to fall upon Him [the Messiah].*

In the life of Abel (Adam and Eve's son), we see how God provided atonement for *one person* (see Gen. 4:4). On Passover, we see God's atonement for *a family* (see Exod. 12:13).

On Yom Kippur, the Day of Atonement, we see God's provision for *a nation* (see Lev. 16:30).

And, in the Messiah, we see atonement for *all who believe* (have faith) in Him as their personal perfect Passover Lamb (see Isa. 53).

But the critical question is, "How can we know *who* is the true Jewish Messiah?"

In the Scriptures, God gives over 300 prophecies that clearly identify the Messiah. According to the law of compound probabilities, there is only one chance in 33,554,432 that even 25 of these prophecies could be fulfilled by a single person.[1]

Whoever has fulfilled the following prophecies is the true Messiah of Israel. The Messiah would

- be born in Bethlehem of Judah (see Micah 5:1-2).

- be born of a virgin as a miracle sign to the Jewish people (see Isa. 7:14). The Hebrew word for virgin used in Isaiah 7:14 is *almah*. This is translated in some versions of the Bible as "maiden" or "young woman." However, in the Jewish Scriptures, when *almah* is used and read in context, it is almost always clear that it refers to "a virgin." Furthermore, God promised Israel "a sign." It would not be a sign for a normal young maiden to bear a child. It *would* be a sign if a *virgin* gave birth to a child by the hand of God. Please note that the Hebrew name of this Child, *Immanuel*, means, "God with us." This shows His unusual nature. Some stumble at this prophecy because of their lack of faith. God, who put the universe in place, could have easily had a virgin bear a child. Besides, what is that compared to God's marvelous creation of a human being!

- be despised and rejected of men (see Isa. 53:3).

- live a sinless life (see Isa. 53:9).

- be betrayed for 30 pieces of silver (see Zech. 11:12-13).

- die for the sins of the Jewish people and the whole world (see Isa. 53:5-6,8).

- die by crucifixion (see Ps. 22:14-18; Zech. 12:10).

- have his clothing gambled for at the time of His death (see Ps. 22:18).
- come before the destruction of the Second Temple (A.D. 70) (see Dan. 9:24-26).
- arise from the dead (see Ps. 16:10; 110:1).

Only *one man* in history has fulfilled these prophecies. He has changed the calendar and the course of history; and millions of Jews and Gentiles have trusted Him for their personal atonement. His Hebrew name is Yeshua, which means, "salvation." To my non-Jewish friends He is known as "Jesus," which was originally translated from the Greek as Je'sus (hay-SOOS) Christos (CHRIS-tose), and was later anglicized as "Jesus, The Christ," which means, "Salvation, The Messiah"!

When you meet God's requirements concerning Messiah Yeshua, you do not lose your wonderful biblical Jewish heritage; rather, you complete your Judaism by gaining the blood of atonement, gaining the Messiah, and gaining an infinitely more personal relationship with the God of Abraham, Isaac, and Jacob!

However, it is not enough for you just to know intellectually that Yeshua is the Messiah. An act of faith is needed to receive the Messiah's blood of atonement and to enter into God's abundant life. That brings us to Law 5.

Law 5 Gives Man's *Prerogative* (A Free Will Choice)...

...You need to ask Messiah Yeshua into your heart and life in order to have the blood of

atonement and a personal relationship with
God, and to enjoy His abundant life. The
Messiah will not force His way into your life;
He desires to be invited.

Joel 3:5 (2:32 in some versions) states,

> *Whosoever shall call on the name of the Lord*
> *shall be delivered [saved]!*

Salvation means "deliverance" from sin's penalty (separation from God), sin's power (over you), and, someday, from sin's presence (eternal life)!

When you ask Messiah Yeshua into your heart and life, you will receive His atonement and eternal life. As you grow in Him spiritually, you will experience personal peace, joy, happiness, guidance, meaning, purpose, and much more than you could ever imagine.

I Found the Abundant Jewish Life

> *I am come that they might have life, and that they*
> *might have it more abundantly (Messiah Yeshua*
> *in John 10:10 KJV).*

As I studied the prophecies which identified the Messiah, I knew in my heart that only one man in all of history fulfilled them, and He was Yeshua of Nazareth.

Yeshua was born of a virgin in Bethlehem. He lived a sinless life. No one ever found even one sin in Him. History testified that He healed the sick by giving sight to the blind, hearing to the deaf, speech to the dumb, walking to the lame, and cleansing to the lepers. He even raised people from the dead! He was despised and rejected by jealous leaders. He was betrayed for thirty pieces of silver. He died by crucifixion for the sins of the Jewish people and for the whole world. Those who crucified Him gambled for His garments. And He died before the destruction of the Second Temple.

> History testified that He healed the sick by giving sight to the blind, hearing to the deaf, speech to the dumb, walking to the lame, and cleansing to the lepers.

The Prophet Daniel wrote that after the "Anointed One" (the Messiah) was "cut off" (murdered), a Prince would come and destroy the city (Jerusalem) and the Sanctuary (the Temple). After Yeshua's death, Prince Titus and the Roman Legions destroyed the city of Jerusalem and the Second Temple in A.D. 70, exactly as Daniel prophesied. Since the Levitical sacrificial system was no longer available, it meant that God had now provided *once and for all time* a perfect atonement through the blood of Messiah Yeshua—for *all* who would believe (see Dan. 9:24-26)!

Yeshua also arose from the dead as King David prophesied. Flavius Josephus, the primary Jewish and Roman historian of that time, wrote in his *Antiquities of the Jews,*

Now, there was about this time Jesus, a wise man, *if it be lawful to call Him a man,* for He was a doer of wonderful works—a teacher of such men as receive the truth with pleasure.... *He was The Messiah;* and, when Pilate, at the suggestion of the principal men amongst us, had condemned Him to the cross, those that loved Him at the first did not forsake Him, for *He appeared to them alive again the third day* [to over 500 Jewish witnesses], as the divine prophets had foretold these and ten thousand other wonderful things concerning Him![2]

Here I was, faced with a dilemma. How could I, as a Jew, accept Yeshua? Would that make me become a *goy*, a "Gentile?" George Gruen pointed out to me that the hope of the Messiah was not of Gentile, but of Jewish origin. It came from the Jewish Bible, and even today observant Jews recite from Moses Maimonides' *Thirteen Principles of the Jewish Faith*: "I believe with perfect faith in the coming of the Messiah; and though He tarry, I will wait daily for His coming!"[3] The question was not whether accepting Messiah was a "Jewish thing" to do—it definitely was—but, rather, *who* is the Jewish Messiah? I had no doubt about who fulfilled all those prophecies! Besides, accepting a Jewish Messiah out of a Jewish Bible and having the Jewish blood of atonement was a very Jewish thing to do. It did sound very kosher! Then, one day, in the privacy of my home, I got on my knees and prayed:

Dear Heavenly Father, I know that I have sinned against You, and I ask Your forgiveness. Messiah Yeshua, please come into my heart and life, cleanse me with Your precious blood of atonement, and make me a child of God. Thank You for doing this according to Your Word. Amen!

When I prayed that prayer, the lights in my room did not flicker. An angel did not knock on my door with a telegram from God. But the God of Abraham, Isaac, and Jacob came closer than my hands or my breath, and I found a peace that passed all understanding and a joy unspeakable and full of glory!

Since that day in Philadelphia, over 40 years ago, the Messiah has not left me. He is a friend who sticks closer than a brother. Everything that God has promised in His Word has come true—love, peace, joy, forgiveness, happiness, guidance, purpose, and so much more! My mother, Ethel, my sisters, Rose and Joyce, and a number of my relatives and friends also invited the Messiah into their lives!

At the age of 19, I married Audrey Yvonne Kitchen. When Audrey was only 6 years old, she contracted Bulbar Polio, the most deadly of the three types of polio. She was completely paralyzed from her neck down to the soles of her feet. She could not move her arms, hands, or legs. She couldn't even swallow her saliva.

Her parents were not yet believers in Yeshua, but her grandparents were strong Bible believers, and volumes of prayer ascended to the throne of God. God reversed the incurable Bulbar Polio and completely healed Audrey! The doctor said it was a miracle! He said there was no way he could explain her recovery medically.

God graciously extended her life another 44 years. Audrey, who hadn't even been able to swallow her own saliva, was given a lovely singing voice to glorify God. She led a very active life as a wife, a mother of two sons, and an outstanding business administrator. We were married for almost 28 years before Audrey went home to Heaven.

In the fullness of God's time, the Lord brought Sandra Frances Sheskin, a beautiful Jewish woman, into my life. Sandra is a first-generation American, born of Jewish immigrant parents from Poland, and raised in a practicing Orthodox Jewish home. Most of her family members, from both sides, were murdered by the Nazis.

Prior to our marriage, Sandra was the main public spokesperson for the United States government on the History and Heritage of the National Emblem of the U.S.A., The Great Seal of the United States. In that position, Sandra was directly responsible to the Office of the President.

Sandra is a Messianic concert singer and recording artist, having shared her love for Israel and her Messiah from Jerusalem to the White House and around the world—and before as many as a million people "live." Together we have been very involved in bringing our Jewish people out of Russia back to Israel, combating anti-Semitism worldwide, and teaching the Jewish Scriptures.

> **Today, there are tens of thousands of Messianic Jews and hundreds of Messianic Jewish synagogues and congregations where Jewish believers worship, with at least 40 such congregations and fellowships in Israel.**

Today, there are tens of thousands of Messianic Jews and hundreds of Messianic Jewish synagogues and congregations where Jewish believers worship, with at least 40 such congregations and fellowships in Israel. Each year, thousands of Bible believers attend Messianic Jewish conferences. What a joy to be involved in this end-time Messianic Jewish spiritual awakening that God promised our people in Hosea 3:5:

> *Afterward shall the children of Israel return, and seek the Lord their God, and David their king [referring to the Messiah]; and shall fear the Lord and His goodness in the latter days.*

There are so many more wonderful things that the Messiah has done in our lives—answers to prayer, miracles of provision, healings of illnesses, supernatural guidance, and much, much more. It would take volumes to write about it.

I cannot encourage you enough to invite Messiah Yeshua into your heart and life.

> *O taste and see that the Lord is good: blessed is the man that trusteth in Him (Psalm 34:9, verse 8 in some versions). Whosoever shall call on the name of the Lord shall be delivered [saved] (Joel 3:5; 2:32 in some versions).*

Here is how to invite Messiah Yeshua into your heart and life as an act of faith to receive His blood of atonement:

1) *Pray:* Prayer is just talking to God in your own words.

2) *Confess*: Acknowledge to God that you have sinned—broken His Commandments—and that you are truly sorry for it.

3) *Ask* and *Receive*: Ask Messiah Yeshua to come into your heart and life and to cleanse you with His blood of atonement.

4) *Believe*: Thank Him by faith for doing this!

Some people have emotional experiences when they invite the Messiah into their life, and others do not. Just thank Him for coming into your heart, not based on human feelings, but on the authority of the Jewish Bible. This is an act of faith acceptable to God! Here is a sample prayer:

> Dear God, I confess that I have sinned against You, and I'm truly sorry for it. Messiah Yeshua, please come into my heart and life and cleanse me with Your precious blood of atonement. Thank You for doing this according to Your Word. I'll do anything You want me to, with Your help. I really mean it, Lord! In Your Name, Amen!

Does this prayer express the desire of your heart? If it does, pray it *right now*, and the Messiah will enter your life as He promised to in God's Word. (You can take a moment right now and pray this prayer out loud.)

Did you invite Messiah Yeshua into your life? Did you really mean it? Then, where is Yeshua according to the Bible? God's Word says,

> *Behold, I stand at the door [of your heart and*
> *life], and knock: if any man hear My voice, and*
> *open the door [of his heart and life], I will come*
> *in to him, and will sup [fellowship] with him,*
> *and he with Me* (Messiah Yeshua in Revela-
> tion 3:20 KJV).

Either God is the world's greatest liar, or Messiah Yeshua is in your heart right now if you prayed to receive Him!

> *God is not a man, that He should lie; neither the*
> *son of man, that He should repent: hath He said,*
> *and shall He not do it? or hath He spoken, and*
> *shall He not make it good?* (Numbers 23:19).

The moment that you asked Messiah Yeshua into your heart and life as an act of faith, God began to do many wonderful things for you including the following:

1) Your sins were atoned for (covered, forgiven)!

2) You received righteousness (right-standing with God) by faith!

3) You entered into a personal relationship with God and became a child of God!

4) You received eternal life!

5) God's Holy Spirit (*Ruach ha Kodesh*) entered your life to lead you and guide you!

6) You began the abundant life and the exciting adventure for which God created you—to know God and to make Him known!

(If you did not yet ask Messiah Yeshua into your life, ask Him to come in right now, and these wonderful blessings will be yours, too!)

Here's how to grow in God's abundant life:

1) Confess any future sins to God and ask His help to overcome them.

2) Pray to God in the Name of His Son (Yeshua) and praise (thank) Him much.

3) Read God's Word (the Bible) once or more every day. Just as you have three square physical meals daily, you need regular spiritual meals. Before you read, pray for God to show you the truth as you read. He is the Author. It is *His* Book.

4) Memorize as many Bible verses as you can. (Start with the verses in this chapter.)

5) Fellowship at least weekly with other Bible believers.

After trying the best the world has to offer and now walking with the Messiah for more than 40 years, I can honestly say there is nothing that satisfies like knowing God in a personal, intimate way.

Commentary by Sid Roth

Many people say to me, "You have been a Jewish believer in Jesus for more than 30 years. Do you still believe in 'Him' as fervently as you did in the beginning? Don't you doubt the experience you had almost a quarter of a century ago? Don't you think you imagined it?"

If that were my only experience, I would have probably stopped following the Messiah many years ago. But my faith is based on two things: the *Spirit* of God and the *Word* of God.

First, the Spirit of God literally lives inside of me. As I am writing to you, I feel His presence. It's like rivers of living water flowing through my body. It's wonderful. I have never been high on drugs or drunk on alcohol, but I can't imagine any high that could come close to what I am experiencing now. I know God is with me all the time. I have seen sickness leave when I say His Name. I have spoken in a language I had never even *heard* previously, let alone learned, and led a man to know Jesus. I have what the Bible calls a peace that passes human understanding. So when someone asks me, "Don't you think you should forget about this Jesus stuff?" I respond, "It's too late. I've already experienced Him. I know Him!"

Second, my faith is based on the prophecies in the Jewish Scriptures. Most of God's predictions about His Jewish people have already come to pass. We can have full confidence that the remaining prophecies will come true as well.

The Scriptures tell about an event that will cause the prophetic time clock to accelerate. Jeremiah says there will be a large exodus of Jews from the land of the north (north of Israel is the former Soviet Union; see Jer. 16:15). Once this happens, the Jewish people in *all* the nations of the world will return. The prophet Ezekiel says not one will be left in the Diaspora (see Ezek. 39:28).

Isaiah says the Jews from China will return to Israel as a sign of the last days (see Isa. 49:12; *Sinim* is Hebrew for China). Most people have never heard of Chinese Jews. But I have been to Kaifeng, China, and met many Chinese Jews who are in the process of returning to Israel.

How will God cause an American Jew to return to Israel? After all, we would not only have to give up our American lifestyle, we would have to face the unique dangers of living in Israel as well.

Jeremiah 16:16 answers this question. First, there will be a season of mercy. "Fishermen" will gently tell the Jewish people that the floods are coming and the only ark of safety will be in the loving arms of Messiah.

But those who do not heed the warning will become victims of the "hunters." Past generations have seen these hunters: Pharaoh, Haman, Stalin, and Hitler. The only place a Jew will be able to find refuge from the new hunters will be in Israel.

Even so, the Bible says *all* nations will turn against Israel in the last days (see Zech. 14:2). Two-thirds of the Jewish people will perish (see Zech. 13:8).

When no hope is left, the Messiah will fight for Israel (see Zech. 14:3). The nation will repent (see Zech. 12:10) and be cleansed of sin (see Zech. 13:1).

You have two choices:

Either come to know the Messiah now and fulfill your destiny by becoming a champion for God, or believe in Him at the last great battle when He rescues us from destruction. The only problem with the latter choice is most of the Jewish people will perish before the great rescue. I believe most of the American Jews will not recognize the American, anti-Semitic deathtrap until it is too late. That was our fate in Hitler's Germany. And death without forgiveness of sin results in eternal separation from God, with no chance of reversal.

If you are not Jewish, your decision becomes even more critical. As you know, the first followers of Jesus were all Jewish! If you wanted to follow Jesus, the requirement was to convert to traditional Judaism. After Peter had a revelation from God, it was decided a Gentile could believe in Jesus without converting to Judaism. The flood gates were opened, and even more Gentiles than Jews followed the Jewish Messiah. But Jesus said in Luke 21:24 that when Jerusalem was in Jewish hands, it would signify the end of the Gentile age.

Jerusalem is in Jewish possession. *We are at the end of the Gentile age.* Multitudes of Gentiles will still be swept into His Kingdom, but those who resist will harden their hearts, and their love will grow cold. *Time is running short!* Some reading this book will be alive during the apocalyptic disasters predicted in the Bible. Others might die tonight. You don't know when your end will come. Now is the only moment you have for sure. Make it count.

After you have prayed to make the Messiah your Lord, or if you have any questions or want to locate a congregation in your area, please visit my website at:

www.TheyThoughtForThemselves.com

Endnotes

1. See http://www.answers.com/topic/compound-probability.

2. Josephus, *Jewish Antiquities* (Cambridge, MA: Harvard UP, 1998).

3. Moses Maimonides, *The Thirteen Principles of Faith* (Brooklyn, NY: Kol Menachem, 2007).

If you would like more information or to respond
to these stories, please visit Sid Roth's website at
www.TheyThoughtForThemselves.com

America may be your birthplace, but Israel is your inheritance!

Israel is on the Rise

In June 2009 Israel was officially upgraded from an "emerging" to a "developed" economy (highest rank), with a standard of living comparable to many European countries. The Israel Shekel is now one of the world's most stable currencies, fully tradeable on international exchanges. Israel is a hi-tech superpower, ranked by some as #2 in the world. Israel's military was recently ranked as #3 in the world in "combat strength." At 60-plus years old, Israel has the largest Jewish population in the world, with more than one third of the world's Jews now living there.

America is on the Decline

The economy of the U.S. is in serious structural decline. Moral and social standards are in freefall. The dollar is falling and asset values are eroding. Anti-Semitism is increasing. As in Europe, Islam in the U.S. is gaining strength rapidly. The sense of a strong, secure America is fading. You can feel there's been a change.

Israel Needs the American Jews

On September 9, 2001, Moshe Katzav—then President of Israel—called for "one million immigrants from European and American countries." Prime Minister Ariel Sharon said in 2002: "Immigration is the true solution to Israel's security and economic problems. It is a holy work...."

God Wants YOU to Come Home

God, through the Prophet Ezekiel (11:17), said: "Thus saith the Lord GOD; 'I will even gather you from the people, and assemble you out of the countries where ye have been scattered, and I will give you the land of Israel.'" Similar statements about "Aliyah"—the return of the Jewish people to their Land from all the nations where they have been scattered—occur over 60 times in the Hebrew Scriptures.

America may be your birthplace, but Israel is your inheritance!

❖